To Pat and Fred
with love,
Paul and Jemmu

In Humility, Our Savior

PAUL H. DUNN

A S P E N
B O O K S

No portion of this book may be reproduced in any form without
written permission from the publisher,
Aspen Books, 6208 S. Stratler, Murray, UT 84107

Library of Congress Cataloging-in-Publication Data

Dunn, Paul H.
In humility, our Savior / Paul H. Dunn

p.   cm.
ISBN 1-882723-30-9 (hardcover)
1. Spiritual life—Mormon Church. 2. Humility—Christianity. 3.
Mormon Church—Doctrines. 4. Church of Jesus Christ of Latter-day
Saints—Doctrines. 5. Dunn, Paul H. I. Title
BX8656.D85235   1997
241' .4—dc21   97-30635
CIP

Words to "In Humility, Our Savior" by Mabel Jones Gabbott. ʿThe
Church of Jesus Christ of Latter-day Saints. Used by permission.

Cover art: "Moses Conversing with the Lord on Mt. Horeb,"
by Wilson Ong

Jacket photograph by Busath Photography. Used with permission.

In Humility, Our Savior

PAUL H. DUNN

CONTENTS

In Humility, Our Savior

In humility, our Savior,
Grant thy Spirit here, we pray,
As we bless the bread and water
In thy name this holy day.
Let me not forget, O Savior,
Thou didst bleed and die for me
When thy heart was stilled and broken
On the cross at Calvary.

Fill our hearts with sweet forgiving;
Teach us tolerance and love.
Let our prayers find access to thee
In thy holy courts above.
Then, when we have proven worthy
Of thy sacrifice divine,
Lord, let us regain thy presence;
Let thy glory round us shine.

—*Mabel Jones Gabbott*

Preface

Perhaps more articles, hymns, and books have been written on the life and teachings of the Savior than on any other subject. This is as it should be, for no other life has influenced the world quite like his.

Our current hymnbook is filled with powerful sermons enveloped in inspiring and uplifting music. These sermons depict the mission of Christ and his teachings. One of these hymns, "In Humility, Our Savior," a sacred sacramental song, became the inspiration for this book. The hymn contains what I consider to be six godly virtues which, when applied to one's life, will help bring a person closer to the assurance that he can return to the presence of his Heavenly Father. In this book I have devoted a section to the development of each virtue.

This wonderful hymn was written by Mabel

Jones Gabbott who, as a long-standing member of the General Music Committee of the Church and chairman of the Hymnbook Text Committee, contributed a great deal to the initial work on the 1985 hymnal. In addition to the hymn "In Humility, Our Savior," she wrote the text for three other hymns. I am grateful to her for her devotion, talent, and inspiration.

This book is not an official Church publication but does contain the author's thinking about several key virtues found in gospel truths.

I express my deep appreciation to Aspen Books for their professional assistance in making this publication possible.

Once again I am most appreciative to my daughters—Janet Gough, Marsha Winget, Kellie McIntosh— and their families, who continue to provide such wonderful support and encouragement, and to Janet in particular, who has given so generously of her time and her typing and creative skills. As always, I am indebted to my wife, Jeanne, for her constant motivation, many thoughts, and ideas. Her unwavering standard of proper English and her expertise with words have been invaluable to me in the expression of my feelings.

Introduction

Long before our mortal lives commenced on earth, there was a great heavenly conflict. While "the morning stars sang together, and all the sons of God shouted for joy" over our Heavenly Father's plan of salvation (Job 38:7), there were some who chose to believe and accept an opposing philosophy. This introduced a spirit of rebellion.

The scriptures record that "an angel of God [Lucifer] who was in authority in the presence of God rebelled against the Only Begotten Son" (D&C 76:25–26), whom the Father had chosen "to bring to pass the immortality and eternal life of man" (Moses 1:39). As a result, the premortal event which was called the war in heaven resulted in Lucifer and his angels, who lost the encounter, being thrust down from God's presence into the earth.

In time all spirits who accept the Lord's plan are to experience mortality. Thus man and Lucifer are to exist on earth together, their purposes, however, being in complete opposition: Man's purpose is to fulfill the Lord's ultimate intent for him, and the earth was created for his good, growth, and development; Lucifer's objective is to destroy that goodness.

In 1832 Joseph Smith received a vision in which he saw the premortal rebellion of Lucifer, and according to Joseph's account, there was to be a continuation of that conflict to this very day: "Wherefore, he maketh war with the saints of God, and encompasseth them round about. And we saw a vision of the sufferings of those with whom he made war and overcame" (D&C 76:28–30).

Mortality, then, introduced us to pain of all kinds and eventual death, along with many temptations and trials.

Though the conditions of mortality are seemingly harsh, when we come to understand the divine principles of opposition and free agency, which are such vital parts of the plan of salvation and thus to our lives, we marvel and are overjoyed as we once were in the spirit world because of the glorious opportunity the plan provides each of us to become like the Father and to live with him again.

Unfortunately, the purposes of rebellion, evil, and adversity are often misunderstood by the world and can cause bitterness and despair. A correct understanding, however, can give us the advantage of accepting and being grateful for these challenges as means to a divine end. And once we realize the love of our Father and his Son for us and their desire for our eternal happiness, we can feel the peace that comes with knowing that with sincere humility, contrite hearts, and ever abiding faith, we are capable of overcoming all earthly obstacles and fulfilling our divine destinies.

As we learn and grow we discover that no one is exempt from trials. And in my trials throughout life, I have learned that I am nothing without God. Over the years I have experienced acceptance by many and repudiation by a few. I have seen my words lift a congregation, and I have seen the same words, on occasion, used against me. I have been surrounded by many, and I have also walked alone. And in all this I have learned what many before me have come to realize: that the only enduring joy, the only persistent friendship, the only eternal power is in God and his Son, Jesus Christ.

When we compare our finite knowledge and experiences to the infinite and eternal qualities of the Savior, and when we recognize our complete dependence upon him, then humility becomes more than an attitude. It becomes life itself. Every thought, word, and deed begins to issue from it. We become humble because we recognize his absolute truth and unconditional love. We are humble because we know that in the end, greater good will come by trusting in him than in pursuing our own desires or in fleeing our fears. We are humble because we begin to understand that there is no path to eternal joy other than in doing his will.

The battles I have waged in my life, as they are in each of our lives, have been challenging, but throughout all encounters, as I have sought the Lord's help, the Spirit has indicated the course I should pursue, whispering simple yet profound instructions.

During one challenging time, the Spirit reminded me of wise counsel my father had given me years before: "Paul," he had said, "when you go to do battle in the world, fight on the Lord's ground and you'll always win; but if you try to fight on the world's ground, you'll usually lose."

There have been times, however—and, again, these occur in each of our lives—when human instincts seem to dominate these feelings. In fighting many of these conflicts I have wanted to put on my old battle fatigues and counterattack. But, turning again to prayer, the Spirit has been clear as he directed me in the way I should go to handle the particular problem. The Lord is gracious to all who seek him.

I have long believed that the real contention in life is not brother against brother, but rather, good against evil. I know that the kingdom will always endure, whatever the ordeal. I also know that the

Lord's servants on earth will continue to guide and direct the Church in righteousness.

I do not claim to have become an expert on the great virtue of humility. Only the Savior of the world would qualify. I do, however, have a desire to become more like him, and I believe that members of the Church everywhere share a common desire to overcome pride and to acknowledge the greater will of the divine while seeking direction for their lives.

In pursuit of this worthy goal, I propose that we search Sister Gabbott's words in her great hymn, "In Humility, Our Savior," which gives direction for gaining not only humility but also its kindred characteristics. Perhaps we may find not only the complete meaning of humility but also the power to develop such virtues in our lives. As a great man once said, "To know and not to do, is not yet to know."

The hymn speaks of six godly virtues. They are:

1. To become as a little child
2. The language of the Spirit
3. Forgiving others
4. Tolerance
5. Love
6. Regaining the presence of the Lord

I invite the Lord's spirit to attend us as we search for these virtues, and I pray that he will bless us all with stronger desires to become like him.

To Become as a Little Child

"True humility, the highest virtue, mother of them all."
—Tennyson

"The secret of genius," Carlyle, the great essayist, once said, "is to carry the spirit of childhood into old age." The Savior taught: "Ye . . . must become as a little child, or ye can in nowise inherit the kingdom of God" (3 Ne. 11:38). I believe that the spirit of childhood has much to do with humility. Children have open minds, for example. We all know that we should have open minds. As Will Rogers, the philosopher and humorist, once said, "Everybody is ignorant, only on different subjects." It follows, then, that if we're all ignorant on some things, we ought to be cautious about thinking we know everything else.

Because they don't think they know everything, children are teachable. They are open to correction. They are less judgmental about whom they

1

are willing to love, not esteeming one man above his neighbor. They are dependent on parents for guidance, instruction, love, and the necessities of life, and they turn instinctively to a loving parent for comfort and aid. We are all children before the Lord and would do well to let the childlike attributes that accompany humility govern our relationship with him.

Almost all prophets learn these lessons early in their lives. Moses, a figure to whom the Savior likened himself (1 Ne. 22:21), a man who would eventually be translated, was of such a humble spirit that his people said of him, "Moses was very meek, above all the men which were upon the face of the earth" (Num. 12:3). If Moses, who could command the very elements of the earth, was the meekest of all men, how much more readily ought we to see our limitations? For the followers of Christ, the same talents and blessings which might make them great in the eyes of the world can be the very things which make them better able to humbly serve God's children. Surely, this was true of the Master who, as the Son of God, humbly descended below all things that he might lift us up.

Jeremiah once questioned a call from the Lord, saying:

> Lord God! behold, I cannot speak: for I am a child.

But the Lord said unto him, Say not, I am a child: for thou shalt go to all that I shall send thee, and whatsoever I command thee thou shalt speak. (Jer. 1:6–7)

Jeremiah, humble as he was, took courage in this promise from the Lord and drew upon the powers of heaven to become a great statesman and prophet of God. To this day he is considered by some to be the most influential prophet of the Old Testament. The Lord's servants are aware of their weakness before him, and they openly acknowledge their dependence upon him.

I am reminded of Abraham Lincoln, perhaps our most able president, who called for national days of fasting and prayer to entreat the help of our Father in Heaven. This man, who had virtually unprecedented authority as president of the United States, saw himself as incapable without divine assistance. On one occasion, after making a particularly difficult decision concerning the Civil War, he seemed reflective and quiet. One of his advisors said, "I hope the Lord is on our side." President Lincoln shook his head and said: "No, rather, I hope we are on the Lord's side" (*Famous Statements, Speeches, and Stories of Abraham Lincoln.* [Palm Beach, Fla.: John D. Hawkins], 1991).

One of the purest examples of humility that I have ever witnessed personally came from one of our latter-day prophets. About six weeks after I was called to serve as a General Authority, I had an occasion to spend some time alone with President David O. McKay. Coming out of the Church Educational System as I had, I was smart enough to take advantage of this great opportunity. This was during the sixties, and young people around the Church were asking difficult questions. I thought I would share with President McKay a few of those I had been asked and learn the Church's official position on each subject. So, for the better part of an hour, I asked question after question, everything from the age of the earth to the controversial issue of blacks and the priesthood; from the time of Adam and Eve's departure from the Garden to when the spirit enters the body. Much of the time President McKay simply said, "I don't know, I don't know. The Lord has never told us that. Someday we'll probably have an answer."

I was astonished and humbled. I thought, here's the President of the Church, the prophet, seer, and revelator, saying, "I don't know," to questions often asked and discussed by the Saints. The lesson, of course, was that we are not to overly concern ourselves with things that have not been revealed. I was surprised later, however, as I traveled around the Church, to find how many teachers seemed to know more about these things than the prophet did. I could never quite figure out how they thought they had the answers that he had not yet received.

As Saints, we all strive to be humble, but sometimes it can be difficult. There is often a price to pay. An opportunity to willingly pay that price came to me from Elder Harold B. Lee some years ago.

In the sixties the First Presidency instituted a policy regarding all books written by General Authorities. Because the contents of these books are often looked upon by Church members as representing the stand or position of the Church on various gospel subjects, the First Presidency wisely requested that they review the manuscripts before they were published. It so happened that the book I was hoping to publish at the time was among the first to be reviewed under the new policy. I had written on the Beatitudes, attempting to interpret as best I could what the Savior had meant as he gave the Sermon on the Mount. The book was called *What Did He Mean?* and as soon as I had finished my writing, I submitted the manuscript to the First Presidency.

In the meantime, my publishers had accepted the unreviewed manuscript and had begun preparing it for press. They had reviewed it and had found no potential problems. Three or four weeks later I got a call from Elder Harold B. Lee, one of the Twelve at the time. I accepted an invitation to meet with him, at which time he graciously informed me that he had been assigned by the First Presidency to read my manuscript. I was pleased when he said: "I want to compliment you. It's an excellent book, and you have caught the spirit of the Savior in it. It will be a fine contribution." I grew concerned, however, when he added, "But I do have one question."

"Please—what is it?" I asked, my mouth suddenly growing dry.

"It's the title. I just have a question about the title." And with great emphasis he asked, "How do you know what the Savior meant when he gave the Beatitudes in the Sermon on the Mount?"

The significance of the question and its answer hit me like a bolt of lightening. Of course I couldn't know—and I was humbled!

Elder Lee then gently suggested not only that we leave it up to the President of the Church to declare what the Savior meant, but also that I change my book's title.

I did that very thing with great rapidity! A few days later Elder Lee approved the new title, *Meaningful Living*.

My next great challenge was to present the change to the publisher!

A long silence followed my announcement, and I knew there was great concern.

"Could you please say that again?" my publisher asked.

I repeated what I had said. He informed me that the book had already been printed.

Now it was my turn to be silent.

Finally, hoping for a convenient solution, I offered, "Can't we just change the cover?" (which I knew had not yet been printed).

"No, Elder Dunn. Every page of the text has the title in the header. *What Did He Mean?* is on the top of every page of the book."

"I see. How many books did you print?"

"Five thousand."

I took a deep breath and at that moment couldn't think of a word to say.

Finally, we proceeded to realistically discuss the situation in greater detail, during which time he remained gracious and polite, despite the realization that the change would create a loss very hard to recoup.

Lesser individuals and businessmen, for whom money, the bottom line, reigned supreme, might not have handled it in this same way. However, my publisher and the printer chose, after making a courtesy call to Elder Lee, to follow the wisdom of the Lord's anointed. To their company's great credit, they reprinted the book with the new title and destroyed the previous printing. It was an act of faith and humility, and they willingly paid the price.

Augustine was once asked what he considered to be the first word in Christian philosophy. He replied, "Humility." And the second? "Humility." And the third? "Humility." But it is one thing to desire humility and quite another to attain it. In fact, you will never know how much of any gospel virtue you possess until you have to develop it during a crisis. You can't just think about it. You can't imagine situations like the one above to gauge your humility. You must live it. You must go through the fire of adversity to learn how willing you are to do the Lord's will. Life, not one's imagination, is the great measuring stick.

Everyday acts of life reveal who we are. After General Conference one year, the General Authorities and their partners held a social for a time of relaxation and association with one another. The hall had been wonderfully prepared in every detail for the occasion. Even the floors had been polished; everything was in readiness.

The night of the party, an elderly sister, the wife of one of the Brethren, walked into the hall. She had taken only a few steps on the highly polished floor when her feet flew out from under her, and she landed on her back with a terrible thud. Before any of us could move, even those just a few feet away, Elder Harold B. Lee instantly responded and was kneeling at her side, comforting her, holding her head, telling her to stay still. I was amazed at his speed in getting to her. Elder Harold B. Lee—soon to become the prophet, seer, and revelator of the

Lord—had had, with the utmost compassion, sensitivity, and humility, only one concern, the welfare of another human being. We learned later that the woman was unhurt, for which we were all grateful, but the memory of that great servant of the Lord kneeling there on the floor, completely oblivious to anything or anyone else except his friend, will never leave me.

It is difficult to speak of humility without thinking of another great prophet, a man who seemed to embody this virtue in every waking moment. All prophets are filled with a profound sense of meekness, which creates in them a strength and greatness not found in other men, but few souls personify the gift of humility as did President Spencer W. Kimball.

Among their many meetings together, the General Authorities gather monthly to learn from and instruct one another. The prophet presides over these meetings as directed by the Spirit. Immediately following an opening song and prayer on one of these occasions years ago, President Kimball pulled a letter from his stack of papers and looked at it hesitantly for a moment. Then he set it back down. The eyes of all in attendance were on him. He seemed concerned, picked the letter up again, and finally said, "Brethren, I'd like to read a letter I received recently." He unfolded it and started reading. "Dear Bigot Kimball . . ."

No one made a sound. He put the letter down, looked at us, and then softly said, "Brethren, I'm not a bigot," his voice almost cracking. He said the words almost as though he thought he needed to convince us. After a moment, he picked the letter up again and read us the remainder. It had come from an aggravated member who had chosen to attack the Lord's anointed for an imagined slight. The prophet, still troubled, then said to us, "This man has misunderstood my motive."

It moved us all to see him baring his soul. He hadn't had to read that letter to us. None of us would have even known it had been sent. But it had hurt him to be attacked in such a personal way, and in humility he shared this man's complaint with us. President Kimball didn't see himself as greater or more favored of the Lord than anybody else. Rather, he saw himself as a servant of the Lord and the people. He saw himself as a student, always learning, especially from the people he served. What a blessing it was to associate with this kind, gentle, truly humble man.

As I have worked with such great men, I have seen the truth of the profound quote by Sir Francis Bacon: "The less people speak of their greatness, the more we think of it." These are men without guile, without affectation, men who would never draw attention to themselves. Yet at the same time, they possess tremendous strengths. Such men do not judge others who lack comparable humility. President Kimball could have made disparaging comments, at least, about the member who had called him a bigot, but he chose simply to suggest that the man had misunderstood his words.

I think how tender and slow to judge the prophets are. They are human beings with emotions and frailties like the rest of us, but they have allowed this childlike characteristic of the Savior, humility, to enter their souls. They trust in him so explicitly that they have no fear of the world, no fear of embarrassment, no fear of others' opinions. I have found each of them to be examples of pure humility. They don't just teach it—they live it. They personify it, even during life's most trying moments.

I was once assigned to travel to the South Pacific with President Harold B. Lee, who was at the time one of the senior apostles. I was a fairly new General Authority, and in our travels together I was to act as assistant and note-taker to Elder Lee. On the way to our ultimate destination, our flight would stop first in Los Angeles and then in Honolulu. When we arrived at the Los Angeles airport, it was discovered that the plane had developed mechanical difficulties and would have to be delayed.

Elder Lee, learning this, was greatly concerned and said to me, "Paul, it is so important that we get to Honolulu on time because I have been asked by my good friend, President Moody, the Honolulu stake president, to give his wife a blessing at the hospital as soon as we arrive—she is not expected to live, and I must get there!"

I knew that Elder Lee had lost his first wife several years before, so it was natural for him to relate closely to the Moodys' critical situation.

As we waited in the airport for the next two hours, he paced in concern and emotional distress. Eventually, the plane was repaired and we continued on to Hawaii where we were met at the airport gate by one of President Moody's counselors, who was quite noticeably feeling sorrow.

He said, "I'm so sorry to have to inform you that Sister Moody passed away about an hour ago."

Now, all Elder Lee's ever-increasing frustrations about our failure to arrive on time surfaced, and he emphatically exclaimed, "No!" He was hurt, disappointed, and certainly concerned for his friend, but also because he himself had felt a personal determination and responsibility, a need, a desire to do whatever he could to give the appropriate help at this crucial time.

Finally at the hospital, the two close friends embraced and wept.

"You'll stay over and speak at her funeral, won't you?" President Moody asked Elder Lee.

"Of course I will," was the answer, and I could

tell from the forcefulness of his reply that he was determined to be there no matter what happened.

That night we were scheduled to attend the dedication of a new chapel. On the way to the meeting President Lee said to me, "Now, Paul, tonight, if you agree, I'd like to call on Brother Arthur Parker to say a few words. He's the only full-blooded Hawaiian patriarch we have in the Church, and I ordained him many years ago. Would you feel all right if I had him speak?"

I was almost embarrassed by his kindness and his consideration for the fact that, though young, I, too, was a General Authority, and he intended to respect my calling. All I could possibly think of to say was, "Certainly."

After our arrival and the usual greetings at the chapel, the program began. Elder Lee called on Brother Arthur Parker to come forward to speak, and as he came to the stand, I could see that he was a giant of a man—a spiritual giant. He was probably in his sixties, and serenity and happiness radiated from him. As he began to bear powerful testimony, he raised his right arm over his head in emphasis, as a gesture, and at that very moment, he suddenly fell backwards.

I had been around death enough to know that as Brother Parker lay at our feet he was gone. He had probably died before he hit the floor. The chapel was suddenly filled with an air of tension and concern. Elder Lee put his hand on my knee and said, "Now don't move. These are very emotional people, and we don't want to alarm them unduly."

I could see that. Several people had risen to their feet. Others started to come forward, but above all else, Elder Lee wanted to induce this wonderful, but very nervous congregation, into a frame of mind where they could be calmed and taught.

An ambulance took Brother Parker to a hospital, although those of us on the stand already knew the outcome. The ward leader quietly but decisively continued to give the necessary explanations and instructions, and in a short time, the mood in the chapel had become more subdued and all present seemed to feel more reassured.

Then Elder Lee leaned over to me and said, "Now, Paul, I want you to get up and lift their spirits."

I was shocked and almost speechless!

"Elder Lee," I said, "they came to hear you."

He didn't even smile. "You can do it," he said. "You can lift them."

Their stake patriarch had just died in their presence, and earlier a stake president's wife had passed away—now I was counseled to make them feel better! It was one of the most humbling experiences I have ever had! If there had ever been a time I needed the Lord's help, that was it. I am very grateful to say that I did feel the Spirit in abundance, and as I finished speaking, the people seemed to feel more peaceful.

The next day was stake conference, and a larger than normal crowd came out to listen to Elder Lee. The meeting was subdued, of course, with heavy feelings still weighing upon many, but the Spirit was strong. We stayed in Honolulu until Monday for Sister Moody's funeral, and the gathering was so immense that many of the Saints couldn't get into the chapel. A sound system was set up for those who remained outside.

On the way to the chapel, Elder Lee seemed unusually quiet. He was to be the principal speaker, of course, so I assumed he had simply been collecting his thoughts for the talk. Suddenly he said to me, "I can't do it, Paul. This is too much like my wife's funeral." He turned to me, and I could almost imagine the burden he felt. "You'll have to do it," he said.

My heart nearly stopped. "I don't know the family, Elder Lee. You know them, and they love you. They want your counsel!"

"No," he said, barely able to speak. "This is too close. There are too many memories. Just teach the gospel. You'll do fine."

We were still ten minutes away from the stake center, and during those ten minutes it seemed that I prayed more fervently than I ever had before.

When we got there, we were ushered through the crowd and seated on the stand. We had leis around our necks by then, and my heart was pounding like a stampede. The choir sang. The opening prayer was given. The people didn't know that this great man, Elder Lee, was considering not addressing them. They were waiting for the remarks of an apostle of the Lord, one of the wisest men on earth. Somebody began giving the eulogy—I had become too incoherent to remember exactly who—when I felt a tapping on my knee.

Elder Lee was saying something. I motioned for him to repeat it, and he said, "I think I'd better do it." I looked at him with absolute gratitude and said, "I know you should do it!"

I had never felt relief quite as sweet as I did then. Moments later Elder Lee went to the pulpit and looked directly at his friend, President Moody. To the best of my recollection, this is how he began:

"Now, President, if it's all right with you, I'm going to talk directly to you and your family. You and I have known each other for many years. We've both held some responsible positions, and we've both taught the Saints about life and death. But now a change has come into your life, and you no longer can just teach these principles—you are now going to have to live them. You are going to have to have faith that everything you've been taught, and have taught, about life and death is true."

His sermon was a masterpiece. He spoke from the heart. He spoke from experience. The Spirit was upon this future prophet as he shared the words of life with several thousand of the Lord's children. He stood firm and resolute in his convictions of the plan of salvation. He knew the truth and shared it with beauty and power.

The losses of his two choice friends, Sister Moody and Brother Parker, on this unforgettable trip had been very hard on Elder Lee, and from my knowledge of other more heartbreaking personal family losses he had suffered over the years, I realized all too keenly that, despite his prominent position and true righteousness, he himself was not exempt from the full force of human trials and their pain. In a few short years he would become the prophet, seer, and revelator of the Lord, and from my own personal viewpoint, I felt he surely was prepared. He had been emotionally refined. He was undeniably humble and completely dependent on the Lord.

The Lord exempts none from the trials of mortality. I think of Joseph Smith, who lost several children in death, who, though innocent, was forcibly torn from his family and put in jail, who later cried for deliverance only to be told by the Lord that he was not yet as Job and that these things would be for his good. I am reminded of President Kimball, who was called to be the spokesman of the Lord, and yet he had great difficulty speaking. His throat had been ravaged by cancer, and for nearly his entire presidency he could not speak above a whisper. He, too, had had to rely upon the Savior for strength. Each of the presidents of the Church has suffered through his own life's trials. Each has been refined in his faith and spirituality, learning to trust in God for strength and wisdom, even for his very breath.

Yet, in spite of tribulation, the prophets are among the happiest, most peaceful men I have ever known. The sweet humility they possess at all times, and particularly in moments of crisis, defines their entire lives. In watching them serve the Lord, who stands supreme as the example of humility, I have been reminded of his words: "Whosoever therefore shall humble himself as this little child, the same is greatest in the kingdom of heaven" (Matt. 18:4).

Let us then seek to do likewise and become as little children. Let us seek his voice, hear his word, and follow.

We are nothing without him.

The Language of the Spirit

"It matters very little what we are engaged in; it is impossible for us to do right without the guidance of the Almighty."

—John Taylor

I have always had a very practical approach to religion. I view my Heavenly Father and the Savior as family members, as literal beings that I can be very comfortable speaking with. We know that Jesus Christ is our elder brother in the spirit, that he, too, is one of God's children, and this helps me feel a closeness to him. When I pray to our Father in the name of Jesus Christ, I feel as though I am talking, literally, to a close family member.

People have remarked that they have seen me talking to myself while I'm driving down Interstate 15, and they've wondered if I was dictating. I've had to smile. I don't usually dictate in the car, but I do occasionally pray aloud there. When I visit with my Father in Heaven informally, I feel a closeness to him, an accessibility that is both comforting and humbling. Of course, I also seek him out in formal prayer, but there are many moments during those informal prayers when I get impressions and assurances that I know are from him. There is a wonderful feeling associated with them, a feeling I have come to recognize as the signature of his voice.

God speaks to man in a variety of ways. He speaks to us through the scriptures, through our living prophets and leaders. He may speak to us through dreams or visions or promptings. But always, there are hallmarks to his voice that give us certainty in listening and following. We find in his voice a type of quiet joy, a soft, simple reassurance that allows us to feel as well as to hear him.

Sometimes, though, the impressions of the Spirit can be so soft and subtle that we may not recognize them for what they are. I remember clearly watching President David O. McKay on television years ago when one of these impressions came to me. We were living in Southern California at the time, and the prophet had just concluded the Sunday morning session of General Conference. As I went to the television to turn it off, I had a feeling about President McKay that I had not felt before. It was just a flash, just a fleeting sensation, then it was gone. Not half an hour later somebody knocked at our door.

One of our teenage daughters, who usually answered the door, was on the phone, so I went to the door myself and found the fourteen-year-old daughter of our bishop standing breathless on the porch. She and her family lived just around the corner.

"Brother Dunn, Brother Dunn," she began almost frantically, "you'd better call Salt Lake. President McKay's office just called my dad, and they can't get through to you!"

"President McKay is trying to reach me?"

"Yes, right now!"

That flash came back to me again, and this time I recognized it as a brief impression from the Spirit. I managed to persuade my daughter to give up the phone, and I called the Church Administration Building. Claire Middlemiss, President McKay's secretary, came on the line.

"Brother Dunn," she said, "you must have some teenagers who like to talk on the phone. We have tried to call you several times but were unable to get through. President McKay wants to talk to you."

"That's what I understand."

"Just a minute, please."

The next voice that came on the phone was the same one I had heard on TV. "This is David McKay."

"Yes, President. This is Paul Dunn. I just watched you a few minutes ago on TV," and for a moment we exchanged a few pleasantries. Then he said, "The reason I called was to see if you could be in Salt Lake tomorrow morning by eight o'clock."

My mind raced. That was less than twenty hours away. "Well, I don't know if you realize that I'm in California right now."

"I know that. I asked if you could be here by eight in the morning."

Nephi had said something about the Lord not giving commandments that we couldn't fulfill, so I took courage. "Yes, President, I can be there."

"Good. I'll see you then. Good-bye, Brother Dunn." He hung up.

My mind was no longer racing. It had crashed. The prophet, who until that moment, I figured, had probably never known that I existed, wanted to see me, and somehow I had to be at his office by eight o'clock. I explained the situation to Jeanne, my wife, and we called the airlines, but had no luck. Everything was grounded in Salt Lake because of stormy weather. There was nothing else for us to do but drive to Utah! Luckily, it was easy to arrange for our three daughters to remain at home because their grandmother was already there visiting. So we hurriedly packed some suitcases, loaded the car in record time, and took off.

As we settled into the monotony of driving across the desert, the weather suddenly took a bad turn. A terrific wind storm came up and was soon blowing huge amounts of sand across our windshield. Then the rain started to pelt down in torrents so that we could hardly see to drive. While this turmoil was taking place, a thought hit me: "This trip is important."

All the way to Utah, through the rain, slush, and mud, I felt the Spirit whispering the importance of the trip, but I was left without any clue as to its purpose. I finally decided that it might be connected with a missionary study guide I had cowritten for missionaries of the Church in our area. Perhaps the prophet wanted to talk to me about that.

I arrived at President McKay's hotel apartment at five minutes to eight the next morning. I hadn't slept or shaved and was bone weary. I could only imagine what I looked like as I knocked on his door. The President ushered me into his office—he didn't seem to be offended by my somewhat disheveled appearance.

After visiting for a moment about my parents and family, he began, in his inviting but decisive way, to explain his purpose for meeting with me so quickly. "We've lost a great man in Levi Edgar Young, one of the seven Presidents of the Seventy, and I am calling you to fill that position."

I was stunned. "Are you sure?" I had never even served as a bishop or stake president.

He looked into my eyes somewhat sternly. "Brother Dunn, the Lord has called you. I'm very serious."

I could see that he was. In fact, I could suddenly see a lot of things—why the Spirit had given me that special feeling prior to the president's telephone call the day before, why I had been told that the trip was important, and perhaps most significantly, why I had not been told what to expect until getting to Salt Lake. If I had known, I might not have wanted to finish the trip. I was very surprised, and yet a peacefulness now settled over me, accompanied by the deepest sense of humility I had felt in my life to that point. I accepted the call and learned that I would be sustained in the next session of conference. My next thought was probably not from the Spirit: How does one get into the Tabernacle?

The Spirit can be compared to the wind. "The wind bloweth where it listeth, and thou hearest the sound thereof, but canst not tell whence it cometh, and whither it goeth: so is every one that is born of the Spirit" (John 3:8). The Spirit can speak to us in a multitude of ways. It can be a brief whisper, just a breath of wind, so to speak, as was my impression that morning watching conference. It can be a constant breeze, never seeming to end, never changing direction, such as the feeling I had had that my invitation to go to Salt Lake City was important. The voice of the Spirit has many dynamics to it, but soft or loud, brief or long, warm or burning within, it is divine. The challenge we have is to

learn how the Spirit uses these dynamics with each
of us individually.

Some years later I was faced with another
unique situation. I had been asked to speak in the
Sunday morning session of General Conference.
Two of the other speakers that morning were to be
President Hugh B. Brown and Richard L. Evans. As
if I hadn't had challenges enough as a young
General Authority, now I was to speak in the same
session as two of the most beloved and capable
General Authorities in the Church. And, although
speaking before Church audiences had long been
part of my regular activity, I had received this invitation to speak only three days before the talk was
to be given. I sincerely felt that the program, had
there been one, should have read:

Apostle and Orator—Hugh B. Brown
Apostle and Orator—Richard L. Evans
Dumb kid—Paul Dunn

I spent the day agonizing, but this time I
couldn't think of a thing to say. On Friday I sat with
paper and pen, sought the Lord's help in prayer, and
wrote nothing. My mind was blank. I spent all day
Saturday searching for the right topic. All I could
think of was, if I'm speaking with President Brown
and Elder Evans, I'd better have something worth-
while to say. I paced all day, and by Saturday night
I was frantic. My head was in a whirl. I couldn't

even think of a story to tell. Finally, after my family had gone to bed, I stole into the front room and knelt in prayer. "Heavenly Father," I said with all the energy of my heart, "thou knowest I didn't ask for this. Thou didst call me, and now I don't know what to do. I can't get any ideas, and I've got to represent thee and thy Church, and . . ."

The answer was in my mind almost before I was aware of it. There was no voice, no vision, just a comforting feeling—just a soft whisper of divine wind.

"You are not Hugh Brown. You are not Richard Evans. You are Paul, and tomorrow morning you will speak as Paul, and all will be well."

I didn't actually hear the words, but their intent filled me. The pressure left, and peace settled upon me. The next morning I stood at that great pulpit in the Tabernacle and visited with the Saints. I was conscious of the Spirit's presence, and I bore my testimony and felt that I had been heard.

All of the General Authorities have the opportunity to hear and be prompted by the Spirit. It is one of the greatest blessings of full-time service in the kingdom. Especially when calling leaders, the Brethren must rely on the Spirit. More often than not they have never met the individuals being considered, and they are called upon to make the *right* decision as new leaders are chosen. The voice of the Spirit is sure. No man by himself could make such decisions. Only God, working with man through the priesthood, can accomplish this challenge.

I have been in many meetings with stake presidencies where I was the youngest in the room. The other men possessed great wisdom and experience, yet they rightly expected me to give counsel so they might know the Lord's will for them, even for them to set their part of the vineyard in order if necessary. Although I had never been in their positions as stake leaders, the Lord in his love and mercy would expand my knowledge and would give me utterance, as he had done and will do with all the Brethren.

To receive this blessing is to experience a portion of the power of God. One senses his love and his willingness to bless his children. The joy and freedom of submissiveness to the Spirit as it rests upon you is a blessing to be cherished. As the Spirit dwells with you, you begin to discover that humility is a consequence of the Spirit's presence, as well as a prerequisite. Then, viewing humility as a reward, you desire to seek the opportunities for service which invite the Spirit. It is one eternal round: If we are humble, we gain the Spirit; and when we receive the Spirit, we are filled with greater humility.

Usually the Spirit leads us to do rational things, but sometimes it can lead us to do the most unexpected things imaginable. That's when humility really counts. I was once sent to a stake conference in California where many people knew me from my institute and seminary days. I prepared what I thought was a pretty good talk and looked forward to speaking to my friends as a new General Authority. I got to the stand, told a humorous story or two, but could not get to my subject. My mind just went blank. I thought, Come on, Paul. You're prepared. Just give your message. But I couldn't do it. I seemed to wander aimlessly, talking about courtship and temple marriage and worthiness and how to prepare for temple covenants. I sat down after twenty-five or thirty minutes.

I almost said out loud, "You dummy, what did you do that for?" I felt that I had really let the people down.

"That's one of the best talks you ever gave," the stake president whispered to me. I tried not to show my shock. The meeting ended and many thanked me, which is always humbling, but this time I felt it was particularly undeserved. I saw a young couple hanging back while others came up to shake my hand. It seemed that they weren't sure if they wanted to talk to me, so, when nearly everybody was gone, I walked their way to make it a little easier for them. As I drew near them, the young man stepped forward and said, "Elder Dunn, could we visit for a second?"

"Certainly."

The intense look in his eyes seemed to penetrate me. "How did you know what to speak about today?"

I didn't want to burden him with my disappointment, so I said, "I just followed the thoughts as they came to me."

He looked at the young lady by his side, then back to me. "We were on our way to Vegas this morning to get married. Our parents still don't know. But before we left, we found out that you were speaking here, and we thought we'd stop and hear what you had to say. What you did here this morning—what you said was just, well, we've changed our minds. We're going to go back home and do this right."

Their bags were in the car, and they immediately left for home. I never heard from them again, but I had seen their resolve and felt they would do their best to please the Lord. I wondered at the time if the Lord would, in fact, single out a couple that needed special help and impress a General Authority to say things just for them. I have long since learned the answer to that question and have a whole file of talks I've never given to prove it. I'm reminded again of the one and the ninety-nine. The Lord will reach out to all his sheep. For the remainder of the day that I had spoken to those two young people, I felt better about the talk I had given. I honestly had not recognized the Spirit working with me while I was speaking, but I know now that he had been there helping me the whole time.

On another occasion, I was asked to perform a temple sealing for a couple I had never met. They had heard me speak and had requested that I perform the ordinance. I went to the temple at the appointed hour and found them just getting settled in the sealing room. After getting acquainted and visiting with everyone, I turned my attention to the bride and groom. Almost immediately I felt that something was amiss. Neither of them would look at me. The groom studied the floor, and the bride looked away from me. They were both turned slightly away from each other.

Usually the groom sits about as tall as John Wayne and knows he's marrying the prettiest girl in the universe, and the bride is just beaming. This is her happiest day, and she radiates just about all the joy a person could have in this world.

But the Spirit just wasn't there, and I wondered what I should do. I usually counsel with the couple for a few minutes first, so I used that opportunity to buy some time. I talked about relationships, first about our relationship with the Lord, then about our relationships at home and what it takes to build a family. Suddenly a thought came to me: Talk about worthiness.

But that's the bishop's responsibility, I thought

to myself. The two bishops and stake presidents involved have signed temple recommends, and it's my duty to honor them. But the impression stayed with me, so I alluded to the fact that we need to be worthy to enter the temple, then moved on. The impression hit me again: Talk about worthiness, and I thought, no, this isn't the place, but an opportunity seemed to present itself, so I spoke at greater length about the subject, then moved on again. The Spirit said a third time: "Talk about worthiness."

I was arguing with myself now. I had spoken of it twice already and nothing had happened. But the impression was strong, so I spoke of it again. I discussed the need for chastity before marriage and then happened to catch a glimpse of the bride's mother. She seemed concerned. Her face seemed to say: "You've already made your point, now move on!" I finished and paused.

The groom took the bride's hand for the first time and said, "Shall we tell him?"

She nodded but didn't say anything.

I stepped a little closer to them and said softly, "Would you like to step into the hall for a minute?" They nodded and stood up. I excused the three of us from the room, caught the mortified looks of both sets of parents, and led the couple into the hallway. A sealing room next to ours was empty, so I invited them in there.

As I closed the door, the groom said, "How did you know?"

I felt no judgment, no condemnation. The Spirit remained with me as I said, "Young man, all I can tell you is that the Spirit is not in your favor. I don't know what you've done, although I'm a pretty good guesser."

They were quiet a moment, then the groom said, "We shouldn't be here. We've been together physically." The bride kept her head bowed and silently wept.

"Well," I said, "I'm grateful for your courage. What do you want me to do?"

They were quiet.

"We can go back in there," I said, "and I can perform this wedding ceremony because I am legally authorized to do so. You will be legally wed by civil law, but God won't recognize the marriage—it won't yet be eternal. You have to understand that God operates by law, and he has decreed that certain conditions must exist before he can seal a couple together for eternity. The Holy Spirit of Promise must ratify this marriage. He has the responsibility as a member of the Godhead to search your hearts and determine if you're worthy to receive this eternal priesthood seal. Only you can answer that. So, what would you like me to do?"

He turned to his bride-to-be and said, "We want to do it right, don't we?"

She hadn't said a word the entire time, and even now all she could do in her state of emotion was to nod her head in agreement.

He looked right at me. "I'm basically the problem. So let's go back in there, and I'll take care of it."

"You don't have to confess anything to them," I said. And then I asked, "Do you have a reception tonight?"

"Yes, for five hundred people."

My heart went out to them. The social pressure in the Church can be enormous, and these two young people were going to feel the full weight of it. "All right," I said, "welcome to manhood. I'm proud of you."

We had been gone for several minutes, and as we went back into the room, every head turned toward us. You could have sliced the tension with a knife. We closed the door, and the groom stood next to me. "Mom, Dad," he began, and he looked at her parents too, "we're sorry, but there won't be a wedding today." A lull filled the room, and then the tears flowed freely.

That took courage. But the couple really had no other *eternal* choice. Once they had entered the temple that day, where they obviously felt terribly uncomfortable, they had begun to see that. But I have often wondered if they would have stopped me without the intervention of the Spirit.

One year later, we met in that same sealing room, and this beautiful couple was sealed for time and all eternity. They radiated. He stood as tall as John Wayne. She glowed with joy. And as the Spirit bore witness to me, I said, "The Lord is here today."

They were sealed, not because I had performed the sealing, but because the Holy Spirit of Promise had found them worthy and had united them for all eternity.

President Kimball was once asked what he remembered as being the most difficult thing he had ever done. After considerable thought he said, "Learning the language of the Spirit." I think many Latter-day Saints would agree with that in their own lives. The Spirit, like the wind, can come to us in many ways. It has greater range than any human voice and greater power than any storm, and yet it can be as soft and gentle as the faintest whisper. It comes to the humble and faithful. It is the power by which angels speak. It is the purest language known and, sometimes, the most difficult to understand. But God is merciful. He knows our weaknesses, and as a loving parent, he will not cease reaching for us until we have turned altogether from him. His Spirit will continue to whisper to us, to guide us and bless us if we will at least try to listen.

I am still trying. I am still listening. And when I have sought him diligently in humility and prayer,

I hear the music of the most beautiful wind known to man. Even in my weakness I hear the whisper of his love. He will always grant his Spirit to guide and guard us if we will try to listen to his divine voice.

Forgiving Others

*Should we even forgive our brother, or even our enemy,
before he repent or ask forgiveness, our Heavenly Father
would be equally as merciful unto us.*

—Joseph Smith

Perhaps one of the best gauges of a person's humility
is his willingness to forgive those who have
wronged him. Offenses will come, says the Lord,
but though they come, it is required that we forgive
all men their trespasses against us (see Matt. 18:7;
D&C 64:10). Can we truly forgive all men for hurting and wronging us, or do we hold on to those
hurts, nursing them until they rear their heads in
new and even more vile offenses, thus perpetuating
and magnifying the original transgression?

Brigham Young knew a thing or two about
offenses. During the winter of 1838, he oversaw the
evacuation of the Saints from Missouri. As men,
women, and children died from exposure and dis-
ease, this great leader, then the President of the
Council of the Twelve, brought order and direction

to the homeless masses pouring into Illinois. He arranged for the support and defense of the Saints, giving his all to alleviate the suffering of those around him. If ever a man saw offense given, it was Brigham Young. Nevertheless, years later he made this remarkable statement: "He who takes offense when no offense is intended is a fool, and he who takes offense when offense is intended is usually a fool." Brigham Young, for all his greatness in leading men, was also a man of contrition and humility. He understood the principle of forgiveness.

Although Joseph Smith was incarcerated in Liberty Jail during the time of the Saints' exodus from Missouri, he was painfully aware of the privations of his people. He knew that no religious group in our nation had ever suffered as the Saints had suffered. Nevertheless, shortly before he died, he declared that his heart was "void of offense towards . . . all men" (D&C 135:4). He was "calm as a summer's morning," without guilt, without doubt, also without anger or any lingering bitterness for the great offenses that had come to him and his people. His brother Hyrum had read aloud the poignant words of Ether just before his death: "And now I . . . bid farewell unto the Gentiles, yea, and also unto my brethren whom I love, until we shall meet before the judgment-seat of Christ, where all men shall know that my garments are not spotted with your blood" (Ether 12:38).

There was no railing, no bitter accusation. Joseph and Hyrum expressed calmness and love for all before their lives were taken. They refused to harbor anger. They refused to accuse. They did more than turn the other cheek; they gave their lives.

"And forgive us our debts, as we forgive our debtors," said the Savior, who had never wronged a soul. "And lead us not into temptation, but deliver us from evil: For thine is the kingdom, and the power, and the glory, for ever. Amen" (Matt. 6:12–13). Before we look to accuse, perhaps we should check our own souls for wrongdoing. All too often, and this principle is frequently misunderstood, the greater offense lies in us for simply refusing to forgive the person who has wronged us. In other words, although our lives may be spotless in every other aspect, if we cannot find it in our hearts to forgive those who have offended us, even deeply, we stand convicted of the greater sin. The Lord tells us: "Wherefore, I say unto you, that ye ought to forgive one another; for he that forgiveth not his brother his trespasses standeth condemned before the Lord; for there remaineth in him the greater sin" (D&C 64:9).

The principle of forgiving our offenders seems to stagger some Saints who are otherwise true followers of the gospel. We are never justified in refusing to forgive. Again the Savior said: "I, the Lord, will forgive whom I will forgive, but of you it is required to forgive all men" (D&C 64:10). We must forgive, but as most of us know, the submissiveness required to let go of offense can momentarily create a bitterness more galling than the original offense. The natural man is strong. But this brief welling up of anger and obstinacy passes if we are humble, and then, if endured, the pain of swallowing our pride will quickly give way to a peace that defies description. Once the eternal desires of the spirit prevail over pride and anger, we can be, and will be, filled with the love of the Creator, which is "most desirable above all things" and "most joyous to the soul" (1 Ne. 11:22–23). Remember, in our great hymn we implore the Lord to "fill our hearts with sweet forgiving." Forgiveness *is* sweet when given unconditionally in the spirit of the Lord.

I recall a good member of the Church who came face to face with this principle in a rather dramatic way. Once while I was presiding at a stake conference, one of the counselors in the stake presidency was conducting the sustaining of general and local officers. As he got to the stake officers, an objection was raised by a man near the front of the chapel. He stated aloud that he was opposed to a member of the stake presidency.

When an objection is voiced in a meeting, the presiding authority has the responsibility to recognize the concern and to arrange for a meeting with the individual who raised it.

After the session the stake presidency and I met with the brother in question. When asked about his concern, he said with some emotion, "Do you see this man, Elder Dunn? He pointed at the counselor to whom he had objected. "Do you see this man?" he repeated. He was becoming red in the face, and I was concerned that he might get out of control emotionally. Still pointing, he shouted: "I will not sustain this man in this life or in the life to come!"

I think we were all stunned. "I'm sorry to hear that," I said as calmly as I could, "but what is your specific concern?"

His face still flushed, he said, "I've been raised to believe that one of a priesthood holder's most rewarding moments would be when he could ordain his son to the office of an elder in the Melchizedek Priesthood. I've lived worthily, I've taught my son the gospel, and I've waited a long time for this great moment. But this man," he pointed at the counselor again, "this man took the opportunity away from me. He took from me the privilege of ordaining my only son!" I then learned that the ordination had taken place some three months before this particular stake conference and that the young elder had been acting in his new priesthood capacity ever since that time.

The counselor was mortified. I turned to him and saw that he was near tears. "Please forgive me," he pled. "Please forgive me." With a broken heart, he expressed his apology to the distraught father in a most humble way. "I'm new. As you know, I've just recently been put in the stake presidency, and after interviewing your son to receive the Melchizedek Priesthood, I didn't fully understand what I was supposed to do. Instead of inviting your family to attend the ordination and having you ordain your son, I went ahead and did it right then under the umbrella of the stake presidency. (The stake president later had it ratified in a priesthood meeting.) I'm terribly sorry. Please, *please* forgive me."

An unfortunate mistake had been made, and I silently asked for wisdom from the Lord. I understood that the counselor had meant no harm, but a great offense had been given, and at that point, I could see no way to undo it or make restitution. I turned to the offended man and said, "I can understand your frustration and concern, but what's done is done. Let's see if we can't, in the spirit of the gospel, work this thing through."

"No," he declared, and he turned to the counselor again and said, "I have the right and privilege of never forgiving you!"

The room was still. I had never experienced this kind of attitude before. "I feel sorry for you," I finally said. "The spirit of the gospel compels us to forgive, not to hate."

"But I have the privilege of not supporting this man," he said. "He has wronged me and my family, and I now have the right of not forgiving."

The counselor was shattered. He had not stopped showing his remorse since the accusations had begun. My heart ached for him. He was obviously a good man who had acted in good faith, and his penitence could not have been more sincere or complete.

"Please," I said, urging the brother to see reason, "there is nothing anybody can do to set this right— except you. You must find it in your heart to forgive this man and put the situation behind you. This leader has made a mistake, but it was done in innocence, without any intent to do harm, and I believe he has done all he can to seek forgiveness—especially your forgiveness. Please," I implored, "please try to forgive him and simply move on."

"No," he declared as defiantly as ever. "I want the privilege of not forgiving him."

There was nothing more I could do under the circumstances. The stake president and other counselor likewise seemed to be at an end of their resources. We excused the father and visited with the dejected counselor, giving him what comfort we could, but he was almost beyond solace. When I got on the plane later that day, I, too, was miserable. I had never seen the spirit of contention so prevalent in an active member of the Church. That father needs help, I thought. *He really needs help.*

On the plane an idea came to me. It was simply a scripture on forgiveness, and I decided that I would share it with the offended father. So the next day I wrote him a short note, quoted the scripture, and mailed the note to him. The day after that another thought occurred to me, with another verse, so I jotted that down also and sent it to him. The third day I thought of something else, and I sent that. The thoughts were simple, to the effect of—"I've been thinking of you today, and I want you to know that I understand your grief. You certainly have the right to be concerned, but please know that this is what the Lord might do." Then I would quote the scripture. I sent a new letter every day for nearly a month.

After several weeks I got a phone call. It was the father of the new elder, and his voice seemed different, softer. "You win," he said. "I can now forgive. Thank you. Thank you."

I hadn't won. The Spirit had prevailed. Somehow as the days had passed and the letters had kept coming, the man had been touched by the tender promptings of the Holy Spirit. Incredibly, where rocklike hate had encrusted his soul, a love and humility now filled him. He openly forgave the counselor for any offense and asked, in return, that forgiveness be extended to himself. His heart had been changed. That is the spirit and power of the gospel. Love and humility had replaced hate.

The Lord is the real judge when differences between people are involved. We cannot presume to know the hearts of our brothers and sisters unless that knowledge is given by the Holy Spirit. There are mysteries in each heart that only the Lord comprehends. "Judge not," he said, "that ye be not judged" (3 Ne. 14:1–2). And through another great prophet the Lord said, "Now it is better that a man should be judged of God than of man, for the judgments of God are always just, but the judgments of man are not always just" (Mosiah 29:12). Leaving judgment to Christ, though, can try even the best of Saints. During the Lord's ministry, even the Twelve struggled with this commandment. "My disciples, in days of old, sought occasion against one another and forgave not one another in their hearts; and for this evil they were afflicted and sorely chastened" (D&C 64:8), and as surely as night follows day, we, too, will be "sorely chastened" if we do not forgive all men in our hearts.

It's a fact that from time to time in our lives most of us will be confronted, in varying degrees, by those who would contend against us for one reason or another, people who will take issue with our values, our points of view, our decisions, some even to the point of conflict. It then becomes our challenge to follow the wise counsel of the Lord when he taught, "Love your enemies, bless them that curse you, do good to them that hate you, and pray for them which despitefully use you, and persecute you" (Matt. 5:44) and "I, the Lord, will forgive whom I will forgive, but of you it is required to forgive all men" (D&C 64:10). We cannot change the hearts of those who disagree with or oppose us, but we can work on our own hearts.

It is also valuable to remember that, not only will we be hurt at one time or another, but that in our human weaknesses we will all hurt others, as well. Remarkably, however, these instances of pain can be transformed into moments of great spiritual growth. We might even call them growth spurts if, in humility, we seek our Savior and allow his Spirit to lead us toward our loving and forgiving others and our being forgiven.

Though knowing and understanding the Savior's counsel, it is still difficult for most to reach perfection living it, but it is possible for us to move closer to that end with his help. In doing so, we release our souls from bondage, for we are then able, with repentance, to be freely forgiven by the Lord. And there is no joy that compares with that of receiving his love. Let us all strive to love and forgive and allow our souls to receive the warmth of his love forever.

Tolerance

Every man should keep a fair-sized cemetery in which to bury the faults of his friends.

—Henry Ward Beecher

Have you ever been misjudged? It's hard to take, isn't it? And when it does occur, we might think it's about the worst thing that could happen, yet there *is* something more unfortunate—and that is to be the one doing the misjudging!

Throughout our lives there will inevitably be times when those who are not able to see into our hearts or understand our actions or motives will misinterpret the things we say or do. Technically, that's all right, for we can learn tolerance and patience from such experiences. Though we might feel pain or even heartbreak, in the long run, hard as it might be, most of us could handle it. But the thing we must become so aware of is that, in spite of the great discomfort being mistaken brings to us, we ourselves are so often guilty of misjudging

47

others, the very thing we so dislike having happen to us.

The Lord has counseled, "Judge not according to the appearance, but judge righteous judgment" (John 7:24). Although as human beings that is often hard to do, hard to understand the "why" of so many things, sometimes if we try to become sensitive to the need, the "why" can be discovered. The principal of an elementary school learned this from experience.

It was the first day of school—at a large school—for Jim, a young Indian boy. He had enrolled late and therefore had to be escorted from the administration office to his classroom by the school principal. As Jim and the principal moved down the long hall, the boy scarcely spoke, and he never smiled. In fact, he lagged behind the principal the whole way, and when asked to hurry, he didn't seem at all responsive. Finally, the two reached the classroom. The principal introduced Jim to his teacher and then left the room.

Upon his return to the administration office, the principal was asked by his assistant, "Did you get him settled?"

"Yes," was the reply, accompanied by a sigh of relief. Then the principal added, "That boy is so slow and backward that I don't think he will do well here."

On the surface, Jim's shuffling behind and unresponsive manner had given the impression of mental slowness, but there was more behind it than that, as the principal discovered the next day when Jim and his teacher came into the office. The teacher announced, "This boy's shoes are too small. He needs new shoes." She had noticed Jim limping, and instead of just "seeing" what he was doing, she asked "why?" His feet were hurting, and when she had him remove his shoes, she saw blisters on the ends of each of his toes.

Of course, the principal, learning this, then saw to it that a doctor was called, the necessary medical attention given, and new well-fitted shoes arranged for. Jim became a different person, eventually turning out to be one of the happiest and most active boys in the school.

Yes, there is a *big* difference between the "what" and the "why." I believe the mark of a truly sensitive individual is his constant attention to looking for the "whys" rather than just the "whats."

Think with me about the experience of a small, assertive man named Zacchaeus. He was despised because of his occupation. He collected taxes for the Roman government. No one liked what he did, nor did they particularly like him. One day he learned that the Lord Jesus Christ was coming to his village, and he wanted more than anything to see him. He raced ahead of the crowd, climbed a tree, and waited for Jesus to pass by.

Now, from this brief verbal description of the man, do you think you would want him for a friend? What kind of man do you think he was, this individual who represented Rome? If you were a Jew you might not choose him as a neighbor.

When Jesus came to the place where Zaccheus was watching from his perch, he looked up and said, "Zaccheus, make haste, and come down; for to day I must abide at thy house" (Luke 19:5).

Jesus didn't just see this little man as somebody who climbed a tree, someone who was disliked. He saw beyond his undesirable occupation, his diminutive size, and his unpopularity and looked upon Zaccheus's heart. He saw a different man than others saw—a man with a sincere desire to do better in the future than he had done in the past. Jesus went to the home of Zaccheus, and there the spark within the small man's heart began to glow more brightly because of the love Jesus had shown him. He had a repentant attitude, and he said, "Behold, Lord, the half of my goods I give to the poor; and if I have taken any thing from any man by false accusation, I restore him fourfold" (Luke 19:8).

We don't know why Zaccheus was collecting taxes. We don't know why he had done some things wrong, but Christ was able to look beyond the outward appearance and look upon this man's heart, and he could see that it was good.

Have you ever noticed that people have a good many problems? The world is full of problems. People don't really want them, but sometimes they actually cause their own because they have made wrong choices, often out of ignorance, sometimes through selfishness. There are always reasons why people act the way they do, and if we can learn the "why," then we can begin to work with those problems and change lives.

So often in dating, young people look upon outward appearance only. It just seems to be our nature to want to be with someone who is beautiful or handsome. And in other instances of judging others around us, it is very natural to see only the exterior, but there comes a time when we need to look beyond the physical and into the heart and the spirit. A classic example of this is the account of the prophet Samuel choosing David to be king of Israel.

Samuel had been told by the Lord to go to the house of Jesse in Bethlehem, and there he would find and anoint a new king to replace Saul. Upon arriving at Jesse's home, Samuel asked that each of Jesse's sons be brought before him. As he looked upon the eldest son, he was impressed with the boy's appearance, for he was tall, strong, and handsome. He had the look of a king. Samuel thought that surely this was the man.

However, the Lord made it known that

although the boy's appearance was impressive, he was not to be chosen. One by one, six more of Jesse's sons were brought before the prophet, and as he looked upon each of them, the Lord indicated that none was the right one.

Then Samuel asked Jesse, "Are here all thy children?" Jesse said, "There remaineth yet the youngest, and, behold, he keepeth the sheep. And Samuel said unto Jesse, Send and fetch him: for we will not sit down till he come hither."

When David entered, the Lord said to Samuel, "Arise, anoint him, for this is he" (1 Sam. 16:1–13).

Why do you suppose the Lord passed over the older brothers and chose the young boy who had not been considered important enough even to be called to the gathering?

Speaking of Jesse's oldest son, the Lord said unto Samuel, "Look not on his countenance, or on the height of his stature; because I have refused him: for the Lord seeth not as man seeth; for man looketh on the outward appearance, but the Lord looketh on the heart" (1 Sam. 16:7).

How much different your life and mine would be if we took the time to pray for the ability to look, not upon the outward image, but upon the heart. How much more we would be able to love our fellowmen. We would tend to be less disgusted with *what* they do, but we would consistently strive to discern *why* they do it.

I believe the secret to happy living is to see beyond the surface and try to understand the "why." While we have been warned about judging our fellowmen unrighteously, the Lord has advised us that we should make "righteous" judgment. I believe a righteous judgment is that which we make when we have the proper spirit and see the inner man or woman, and there find that spark that Jesus found in Zacchaeus, and indeed finds in all mankind.

Solomon once said, "He that is slow to wrath is of great understanding: but he that is hasty of spirit exalteth folly" (Prov. 14:29). It seems to me that patience, understanding, and compassion play a crucial part in our ability to be tolerant. If we are to allow others to be who they are without condemning them (a sign of tolerance), a measure of patience is usually required. Being "slow to wrath" or in any way hasty in our judgments gives us the time to find acceptance in our hearts for others—not that we accept their false beliefs or sinful or destructive ways, but that we accept them as our brothers and sisters, as children of our God. Such tolerance requires patience, humility, long-suffering, kindness.

Years ago in Southern California, I had an experience which I remember clearly as one of my most cherished spiritual encounters. The Institute of Religion building on the University of Southern

California campus was relatively new. I was the Institute director and coordinator, and my office was located in the building. As a part of my assignment, I was a member of the campus pastor organization. The group consisted of several Protestant ministers, a Roman Catholic father (Newman Club) a Jewish rabbi (Hillel Foundation), and I was the Latter-day Saint representative. We met regularly and discussed issues common to our various programs. We all became good friends and often shared ideas and philosophies. Just down the street from our building was the Hillel building, the Jewish organization headquarters. It was a new facility, also, and was admired by all. The director, a rabbi named Ben, a wonderful teacher and scholar, was my good friend. We had much in common and often shared our joys, successes, and challenges.

One day a fire broke out in the Hillel building's kitchen that caused sufficient damage to make it necessary to close the facility for several weeks in order that repairs could be made. This meant that our Jewish friends would be without a place to meet. I approached my friend Ben and said, "You and your students are welcome to use our Institute of Religion building until your building is renovated, without charge, of course. All you would have to do is schedule your classes and activities at times that would not conflict with our programs, and otherwise, all I ask, Ben, is that your students maintain LDS standards.

"You would do that for us, Paul?" he responded.

"Why not?" I asked. "We're friends, aren't we?"

"Well, yes," he said, "but we are not of the Christian faith!"

I said, "What does that matter? Our religion teaches the brotherhood of man and the fatherhood of God, and in reality, we are brothers." Tears came to his eyes and we embraced.

As we stood there together, I couldn't help but think of what H. G. Wells, the novelist, philosopher, and historian, once said. Said he, "I am convinced that there is no more evil thing in the present world than race prejudice, none at all! It is the worst single thing in life. It justifies and holds together more baseness, cruelty, and abomination than any sort of terror in the world." And you and I know we have plenty of it in the world and even right here in the United States.

I recall saying to my friend, the rabbi, "Ben, I am a Latter-day Saint and I am proud of it! And I know you are equally proud to be a Jew! I am proud of my distinguishing peculiarities and what sets me apart from others. And yet, like you in Judaism, we Mormons are often misunderstood, persecuted, and sometimes martyred."

He said, "Paul, let me share an experience a rabbi friend of mine had, an experience that spoke about misunderstanding and mistreatment." He related that his friend had received the following correspondence from a Protestant minister.

> Rabbi Mark, I have a confession to make. . . . We have taught our children to hate you because you crucified Christ, neglecting to implicate the Romans and neglecting to add that by the same process of reasoning we ought to hate New Englanders because they are witch burners. . . .
>
> We have made the so-called Christian centuries a night of horror for the Jew. In many states we have put on you the whole burden of taxation. . . .
>
> We have invited you here to our land of free and unlimited opportunity, but some of our schools keep you out and some of our businesses say, "You're not welcome here."
>
> We have damned you for the very attitude which we ourselves have made inevitable. We have robbed you and now criticize you for being secretive. We have driven you together like sheep in a storm and now call you clannish.
>
> We have accused you of materialism, because you have been successful in business. Your prosperity has been evidence of a mercenary mind, ours an evidence of the favor of God. . . .
>
> One of the controlling spirits of the world's life has been yours. The Greek gave us thought; the Hebrew intuition; the Greek, nature; the Hebrew,

God. We speak of the Hebrew Spirit, but we have not bowed to you in token of our debt. . . .

We have appropriated your heroes bodily. We can have no marriages without your Mendelssohn, no story of philosophy without your Spinoza, no anthology of verse without your Heine. Our Victorian Age lacks its chief ornament without your Disraeli. And today we have the benefit of your Brandeis in jurisprudence, your Strauss and Rosenwald in philanthropy, your Flexner and Einstein in science.

We have laid violent hands upon your saints. We stole the massive Moses, the flaming Elijah, the knightly David; and that most august group in all the succession of those who have declared God—the prophets. The mind lifts at the call of their names—Amos, Hosea, Micah, Isaiah, Jeremiah. The rapt John was yours, and that apostle, who after the cornerstone was laid, built the Christian church. He was yours, in whose face we have seen God supremely. He was born of a Jewish woman, nourished at a Jewish breast, nurtured in a Jewish home, led by Jewish teachers, set aflame at Jewish altars. . . .

Rabbi Mark, you are a Jew and I am a Christian. An ocean rolls between us. Let us make it not a barrier, but a highway. You must go on saying: "Hear, O Israel, the Lord our God is one Lord." We must chant still: "Worthy is the Lamb that was slain to receive power and riches and wisdom and

strength and honor and glory and blessing." But
shall we not together say: "Behold how good and
how pleasant it is for brethren to dwell together in
unity"; and "glory to God in the highest and on
earth peace among men of goodwill?"

I thanked Ben for sharing that special experience and all the while pondered the treatment of
his people in that horrible holocaust at the hands of
Adolph Hitler.

Do you think, in view of the many and great
contributions the Jews have made through the
prophets, great statesmen, musicians, and other
leaders, that we can treat them, or any of God's
children, with disdain and still call ourselves good
Christians and citizens?

While many years have passed since those
delightful days on campus, I still feel that warm
glow and inner peace when I think of my good
friend, Ben—the Jew.

During the Savior's ministry, a woman who had
committed adultery was brought to him. No doubt
she was an Israelite who was expected to follow the
teachings of Moses. Jesus knew her sin, and he
knew the hearts of those who had brought her to
him. According to the law, they were authorized to
stone her to death, but Jesus, in his divine wisdom
and benevolence, suggested that "he that is without
sin among you, let him first cast a stone at her." The

accusers were "convicted by their own conscience" and left the scene. Then, when only the Master and the woman were left standing there, she stood dumb before him, amazed, and the Savior inquired: "Hath no man condemned thee?"

"No man, Lord," she responded, beginning to recognize his position among the sons of men. And he kindly replied: "Neither do I condemn thee: go, and sin no more" (John 8:3–11). He did not embarrass her. He did not accuse her. Although her sin was "as scarlet," he knew that she could yet be made "white as snow" (see Isa. 1:18). He did not say that she was forgiven yet, perhaps because her repentance was not yet complete, but through his kindness and love, he invited her to come to truth and "sin no more."

How great a tool compassion is. How marvelous are the effects of "gentleness, meekness, and love unfeigned."

Out of some two hundred missionaries who might be serving in an LDS mission at any one time, there are always a few that will present a challenge. Shortly after we arrived in New England to begin my assignment as mission president, I received a call from a missionary who had come just the month before. He had previously gone through some difficulties at home, although he had a wonderful family. During my first meeting with him, he explained that he hadn't really wanted to go on a mission in the first place, but did so to please others. He said he wanted to return home. In fact, his comment was:

"I don't like my mission.
I don't like New England.
And already I don't like you.
Send me home."

I simply said, "I'm grateful for your candor, but you should know that in the few weeks I've been here,

"I love the Lord and my mission.
I love New England.
And I think you have great potential."

Somehow by giving him lots of encouragement in that first meeting, I managed to convince him that the better part of wisdom would be to change his mind about going home and stay right where he was, which he did. But every time we sat together, he continued making negative statements. Near the end of his mission, however, he completed learning the material he was responsible for, and I was able to make him a senior companion. Finally, the last week of his missionary service came, and as part of our procedure when missionaries were ready to return home, he came into the mission home with several other elders who were also leaving to spend his last night. We all had dinner together, then held a farewell testimony meeting for the group. During that session he stood and reported, with much emotion,

> "I love the Lord and my mission.
> I love New England.
> And President Dunn, I kinda like you!"

I realized once again that which I had seen so many times before—the value of patience and tolerance. I don't think that hearts can be changed by harshness and pounding the pulpit, but patience and tolerance combined with love can help both sides understand each other.

Obedience cannot be forced on any soul. As testimony holders we can lead; we can persuade; we can implore; we can motivate; but we must never force. The sacred direction of the Spirit is real, but for those who do not yet feel it, or do not choose to follow it, we can only pray and serve and befriend. Even when others' disobedience offends us, we should be tolerant and patient, within reason.

Would we wish to do any less than that which our Father does himself? The hymn "Know This, That Every Soul Is Free" reminds us of his technique for honoring the free will and choice of each of his children.

> Know this, that every soul is free
> To choose his life and what he'll be;
> For this eternal truth is given:
> That God will force no man to heav'n.
>
> He'll call, persuade, direct aright,
> And bless with wisdom, love, and light,
> In nameless ways be good and kind,
> But never force the human mind.

When the Savior came to the Americas after his resurrection, he said:

> And there shall be no disputations among you, as there have hitherto been; neither shall there be disputations among you concerning the points of my doctrine, as there have hitherto been.
>
> For verily, verily I say unto you, he that hath the spirit of contention is not of me, but is of the devil, who is the father of contention, and he stirreth up the hearts of men to contend with anger, one with another.
>
> Behold, this is not my doctrine, to stir up the hearts of men with anger, one against another; but this is my doctrine, that such things should be done away. (3 Ne. 11:28–30)

To rephrase this, I would say the Lord wants us to have tolerance for one another, even in our weaknesses and differences, and to learn to love and work together. If we do this, we just might find that our differences are reasons for rejoicing rather than contending with each other.

The gospel of Jesus Christ is the greatest news the world has ever heard, but many of our Father's children are not prepared for it at this time, and others won't listen to it unless it comes to them in a package of love and tolerance for who they are. This can challenge us as Saints who know the truth and can see the changes they ought to make in their lives. To tolerate others is not necessarily to agree with them; it is not to compromise with them; it is not to accept their falsehoods or negative ways of life; but it is to accept them as sons and daughters of God. It is to love them unconditionally, even as Christ loves them. It is to be humble as we listen to them, teach them, have patience with them, as we empathize with their pains, even when we know their pains come from sin or unwise choices.

To be tolerant means looking beyond differences in people and recognizing the divine potential in every individual. To be tolerant means finding pur-poses and ideals that we have in common and in those things, participate wholeheartedly. We do not seek to condemn others for their differences, but, rather, to offer them our appreciation, love, and friendship.

A message on tolerance and love from one of the Savior's parables was put in a quatrain, a stanza of four lines:

The Jew had drawn a circle that shut him out,
Heretic, rebel, a thing to flout.
But a certain Samaritan had the courtesy to win,
He drew a circle that took him in.

I am reminded of an experience I once had in a barbershop. The two barbers there had worked side by side for twenty years, and in all that time they hadn't seemed to agree on much of anything. Everything they discussed seemed to turn into a debate, as they pitted one against the other. Finally, interrupting another one of their arguments, I said to them, "You two seem to disagree about everything. You'd even argue about whether the sun was up. Why don't you just find different places to work and be free of each other?" The barbers looked at each other, astonished. Then one of them said to me, "You don't understand. We've been friends for twenty years. We differ in our heads, but we're buddies in our hearts."

These two men understood that their opinions were not as important as their friendship.

I believe that tolerance is necessary if we're going to love someone we disagree with. To be able to overlook differences, even significant differences, so that we can cooperate with others is a mark of maturity. Too often we hear the refrain: "I will not tolerate this!" That comment reminds me of a little child who picks up his toys and goes home because he gets his feelings hurt. Wouldn't our relationships be more productive and peaceful if we forgave one another our trespasses, overlooked each other's lack of understanding, and focused on the divine worth of each soul? Jesus had faith in the worst of men because he saw the possible best in them.

Our entire society would be elevated if we lived by the motto one group tried to follow: "Agree to differ; resolve to love; unite to serve."

The hymn I quoted at the beginning of this book implores the Lord to "teach us tolerance and love." Are we willing to listen to him as he teaches us to set aside our pride that we may love one another? Are we willing to receive the friendship of those who do not always please us, who believe and act differently than we do? Are we wise enough to avoid contending with those who would fight us and accuse us? Are we spiritually mature enough to overlook the annoyances and disappointments in our own family members for the sake of greater peace in our homes? How blessed we would be in our marriages, in our relationships with our children, our friends, our neighbors and coworkers, those who serve us in our communities if we would follow this admonition of Paul:

> I therefore . . . beseech you that ye walk worthy of
> the vocation wherewith ye are called,

With all lowliness and meekness, with long-suffering, forbearing one another in love. (Eph. 4:1–2)

Peaceful lives are a mark of true Saints. Let us have tolerance and love for all men, so that the peace we enjoy as Saints may spread wherever we go.

Love

Perfect love casteth out fear
—1 John 4:18

In all the latter-day prophets that I have been privileged to associate with, I have seen the great common denominator of Christlike love. I have found each of them to be filled with this love. Upon meeting President McKay, I felt his sincere concern for my welfare as a young servant in the kingdom. I saw his love of truth and honesty and his deep love for every one of Heavenly Father's creatures. I felt President Lee's immense love for others, his compassion for those who suffered, and of course, his deep love for his family, some of whom had been taken from him. President Kimball's pure and humble love was great enough to affect every person he met. It removed people's fears, comforting the wary and the distrusting. I have known President Hinckley for over thirty years and have worked with him closely. I can speak confidently of his powerful love of Christ; it is his abiding compass. Each of the prophets is filled with the charity of Christ. It is pure. It is strong. It radiates from them. Truly they exemplify John's declaration that "God is love; and he that dwelleth in love dwelleth in God, and God in him" (1 John 4:16).

Prophets are positive thinkers. Their natural enthusiasm for life lifts others and causes them to grow in their own spheres. I am concerned sometimes when I see how we as members, living in a very active world, get bogged down and begin to focus on the negative in our lives rather than the positive. As parents, especially, some of us try to raise our children through negative reinforcement rather than positive.

Researchers have found that between birth and twenty years of age the average child receives over one hundred thousand negative messages, most of them in the home. Hopefully in our Latter-day Saint homes these averages will be more encouraging, but evidence suggests that even among active Church members negative messages in the home often outnumber the positive. We know that most parents love their children, so what can be done to reverse this tide of negative training?

JoAnn Larsen, a knowledgeable and experienced family therapist in Salt Lake City, suggests that we try to develop lenses—vision that sees positives instead of negatives. She believes that miracles would occur in every life if we praised the positives and helped to lift people over obstacles through encouragement. It seems to me that she is asking us to treat difficulties in our lives the way the prophets do—with faith, hope, and love.

I don't know, but it seems to me that living and growing on this earth may in the end be the most difficult thing we are called upon to do in our eternal lives. Most of us are weighted down, sometimes grimly, with the serious tasks of earning livings, of paying mortgages or rent, rearing children, faithfully fulfilling Church callings, attending school, living righteous and worthy lives—the list could go on. Life is serious. Children must be taught, bills must be paid, correct decisions in our lives must be made. We are faced with a never-ending stream of negative forces, and we can't help but worry sometimes, but I wonder if the constant bombardment of dilemmas and challenges doesn't frustrate and depress us to the point where our minds are distracted from the very principles that would allow us to rise above the destructive influences in our lives.

Are we so worried about the Ds our sons may have received in math that we can't praise them for the beautiful smiles on their faces each morning? Are we so worried about paying the rent that we can't share a piece of our hearts with our spouses each day, perhaps simply mentioning that we love them? Adverse forces surround us, but so do positive ones. Maybe we need to take a little time to focus our lenses.

I once read a story which was told by a young businessman. He was opening a new office, and a friend sent a floral arrangement to help him celebrate the occasion. When the friend arrived at the opening, he was appalled to find that the florist had sent a wreath bearing the inscription "Rest in Peace." He went to the florist and complained. After apologizing, the florist said, "Look at it this way. Somewhere today a man was buried under a wreath that said, 'Good luck in your new location'."

This florist had focused his lenses.

Seeking to lift someone is a part of loving. Joseph Smith said, "A man filled with the love of God, is not content with blessing his family alone, but ranges through the whole world, anxious to bless the whole human race" (*History of the Church,* 4:227). All prophets and true Saints are filled with love for others, and that love leads them to bless the lives of all they meet.

Thomas Moore, the famous nineteenth-century Irish poet, epitomized this love. After being gone for some time on business, he returned home to find a doctor at his door.

"Your wife is upstairs," said the doctor, "but she has asked that you not come up." Then he told Moore the terrible truth: his wife had contracted smallpox and her once flawless skin was already pocked and scarred. She had seen herself in the mirror and commanded that the shutters be drawn and that her husband never see her again.

In his love and concern, Moore ignored the decree and ran upstairs and threw her door open. In darkness he groped along the wall for the gas jet that would illuminate the room.

"No!" a startled cry came from a corner of the room. "Don't light the lamps!"

Moore hesitated, swayed by the pleading in her voice.

"Go!" she begged. "Please go! This is the greatest gift I can give you now."

Reluctantly, Moore left the room and closed the door. He went to his study, where he sat up most of the night prayerfully writing. He didn't write a poem this time, but a song, including the music. It was the first song he had ever composed. The next morning at dawn he returned to his wife's room.

In the darkness, he felt his way to a chair and sat down. "Are you awake?" he asked.

"I am," came a voice from the far side of the room. "But you must not ask to see me. You must not press me, Thomas."

"I will sing to you, then," he answered. And so for the first time, Thomas Moore sang to his wife the beautiful song that has endured to this day:

> Believe me, if all those endearing charms
> which I gaze on so fondly today
> were to change by tomorrow and flee in my arms
> like fairy gifts fading away,
> Thou would'st still be adored, as this moment
>   thou art—
> Let thy loveliness fade as it will.
> And around the dear ruin each wish of my heart
> would entwine itself verdantly still—

As the song ended, Moore heard his wife rise. She crossed the room to the window, reached up, and drew open the shutters.

He had lifted her through love. Despite her withdrawal from the world, and even from him, he had reached for her in persuasive, sustaining love. How easy it would have been for him to have faulted her for her fears. But love would not allow that because pure love "suffereth long, and is kind, . . . is not easily provoked, thinketh no evil, and rejoiceth not in iniquity but rejoiceth in the truth, beareth all things, believeth all things, hopeth all things, endureth all things" (Moro. 7:45).

Thomas Moore may not have understood the fullness of the gospel, but he understood and lived the principle of love. We need such understanding in the world. There is the story of the husband and wife who had saved and saved for a new car. After taking delivery, the husband told his wife that all the necessary legal documents and insurance information were in a packet in the glove compartment. On her first day out in the new car, she was involved in an accident which demolished the car's front end. Unhurt, but in tears and near panic, she opened the packet to show the police officers her papers. There she found a handwritten note from her husband. It read: "Now that you have had an accident, remember, I can always replace the car, but not you. Please know how much I love you!"

There is great power in this positive message. Truly, love does "endure all things." A special friend of mine, Dr. Thomas Myers, shared this tender experience:

A small boy accompanied his grandparents into Dr. Myers' medical office. The old man was leaning on the boy's two outstretched hands as he moved. The child encouraged him with, "Come on, Grandpa, you can make it! . . . Only a little farther, Grandpa. . . . The doctor will make your leg better." A sweet grandmother walked behind.

After the visit, the boy and his grandfather exited the same way. The little boy was given a helium balloon on his way out. He helped his grandfather to the car, then ran back in and, pulling himself up to the counter, asked the receptionist, "Please, may I have another balloon?"

His grandmother, still standing there, scolded him, "Of course you can't. I warned you not to let

that balloon go!" She apologized to the receptionist. "He did this last week—went right outside and
let his balloon go. I really did warn him this time."

The little boy was trying to tell her something.
She bent down to listen. Then, with tears showing
on her thin, wrinkled face, the grandmother asked,
"Could he please have another balloon? You see, his
little sister died a few months ago, and he wanted
her to have a balloon to play with, too."

A simple act of love can remind us all of our
greatest purpose in this life—to learn to love as
Christ loved. Is it possible that our initial reactions
to others' mistakes, especially to our children's, may
be the wrong reactions? A positive, loving word can
often correct a mistake while strengthening our
bonds of affection for one another.

It is so easy to make mistakes in our judgments
of others and their actions when we don't understand the surrounding circumstances. Over the
years I have often stressed the importance of keep-
ing a positive attitude and viewpoint as we observe
our fellowmen, wherever they are—in our homes or
elsewhere. The following story relates how one man
learned this lesson.

"When I was young and pretty much satisfied with
myself," an elderly man once told me, "I spent a
college vacation looking for what I called local
color, for use in a book I planned to write. My

main character was to be drawn from an impoverished, shiftless community, and I believed I knew just where to find it!

"Sure enough one day I came upon the place, made to order with its run-down farm, seedy men and washed out women. To top it off, the epitome of the shiftlessness I had envisioned, was waiting for me near an unpainted shack, in the shape of a scraggly-bearded old man in faded overalls who was hoeing around a little patch of potatoes while sitting in a chair.

"I started back to my rooming house, itching to get at my typewriter. As I made the turn in the road which ran past the cabin, I looked at the scene from another angle, and when I did, I saw something which stopped me cold in my tracks. From this side, I observed, leaning against the chair, a pair of crutches, and I noticed one empty overall leg hanging limply to the ground. In that instant the lazy, shiftless character I had seen was transformed into a figure of dauntless courage.

Since then I have not judged another man after only one look or conversation with him, and I thank God that I turned for that second look."

—Author Unknown

It has often been quoted: "Two men look out the same bars: One sees mud, and one see stars" (Frederick Langbridge, in *Oxford Dictionary of Quotations*, 2d ed., London: Oxford University

Press, 1966, p. 310). Judgments must be made at times, but let us also voice our gratitude for the goodness that resides in these same people. Let us recognize the strengths and courage of so many souls, the many wonderful examples of virtuous living, the exceptional talents and achievements of our family members, neighbors and friends, and all those with whom we come in contact. Let us remember to count our blessings and to lift others, to encourage them, to inspire them. Let us especially remember to praise and adore our children.

Love for those who love us is a simple matter compared to loving those who seek to do us harm. We are told to love and forgive our enemies, but true forgiveness cannot be given without the influence of Christlike love. When we cannot love our enemies, we may secretly seek them harm for the harm they have given us. I am reminded of a statement that Heine, the great German poet, once made, indicating that charity still had not found a place in his heart.

> Mine is a most peaceful disposition. My wishes are: a humble cottage with a thatched roof, a good bed, good food, the freshest milk and butter, flowers before my window and a few fine pine trees before my door.
>
> And, if God wants to make my happiness complete, he will grant me the joy of seeing some

six or seven of my enemies hanging from those trees.

Before their deaths I shall, moved in my heart, forgive them all the wrong they did me in my lifetime. One must, it is true, forgive one's enemies—but not before they have been hanged.

I hope Heine made this statement as a tongue-in-cheek way of saying that he had endured much at the hands of his critics—but one cannot be sure. We all have critics. We all have enemies, whether we deserve them or not. I am almost convinced that God allows enemies and critics because they have a right of choice and so that our love can grow, spurred by the fires of affliction.

Toward the end of World War II I had an experience I have often shared where love for my enemies became a reality.

We had just cleared an enemy position on the island of Okinawa, and as my particular squad had been active in taking the hill involved, I was there helping to secure the area and at the same time doing what American soldiers did so well—hunting for souvenirs. While I was busy doing this, I noticed a young enemy soldier lying on a stretcher nearby. He had been wounded and had surrendered. One of our interpreters had been interrogating him, and so before the young soldier was evacuated from the area, I was able to talk to him briefly.

He was seventeen and had already fought for two years in China. He asked if we had bombed Osaka, his hometown. He talked about his family and his dreams. He was an avid sports fan. As I knelt beside him, I was stunned. We were identical in so many ways. I didn't want to fight, and he didn't want to fight. He loved baseball, and I loved baseball. He loved his family, and I loved my family. Had World War II been left to us, we would have shaken hands and gone home.

I will never forget that incident and the lesson of life I learned from seventeen-year-old Matsua Watanabe. Somehow during that memorable conversation I sincerely came to love my "enemy." Also, it was then that I caught the full vision of the fact that the real conflict there was not between people but between ideologies.

Years later I was asked by the First Presidency to tour the Fukuoka Mission, of which Okinawa was a part. This time I went as a representative of the Savior and his church. My wife and I stayed in a hotel that stood near the very spot where I had dug a foxhole and spent my first night on the island. I hadn't slept that first night of battle, and now I couldn't sleep because of the memories. I sat outside on the hotel balcony that night reliving some of the experiences I had faced over two decades earlier. In the ninety days we fought, many thousands of people had died, soldiers and civilians alike. The memories were vivid, unblurred by time. An eeriness settled upon me outside on that balcony as I saw it all again just as if it had been yesterday. At dawn my thoughts came back to my current mission; I was there to visit Okinawan members and our American service personnel.

Following our conference, I asked the mission president if he would drive my wife and me to the area of Shuri Castle, which was the site of one of the most bitter battles of the war. He generously agreed, and a little later a group of us stepped out of the car near the hallowed battleground. Feelings again ran high. Hesitantly, I asked if I could take my wife to see the caves near the castle site where I had once experienced a difficult assignment. I fought emotions as I showed her the spot.

After reflecting a while on these memories as I had done so often in the past, Jeanne and I viewed the rest of the area and then returned to our host and our driver, the branch president. I noticed in the branch president a tenseness, and I asked the mission president if I had caused a problem. He said, "Please don't worry. This is a very sacred place to him. He lost his father and older brother near here." On such occasions as this, one appreciates the deep meaning of the brotherhood of man and the assurance of the hereafter.

At that moment, also, another vivid picture came to my mind. Earlier that same day at our conference meetings, as my wife and I were sitting on the stand, we both made a startling observation, one which will always burn brightly in our minds. There on the stand together, presiding, conducting, and participating in the service, were an American Church leader, an Okinawan branch president, and a native Japanese mission president, all of whom had been somewhere in the area functioning in some capacity in the days of World War II. And sitting in the congregation in front of us were a great many Okinawans, some of whom had lived on the island during that war period, or their descendants, along with a large group of American service personnel who would in a way be representing the armed services of days gone by. All except a few visitors were Latter-day Saints, happy and excited to be together, with a strong spirit of friendship, companionship and bonding, and love present. Indeed, we were "one" as a group.

Under the particular circumstances of most of those present, the whole scenario was amazing. And I can't think that the unbelievability of the event could have been lost on many, especially those who had been alive in earlier years. It was a testimony, of course, of what knowing the truth and acting upon gospel principles can do in our lives if we are willing.

My wife and I were very impressed also with the fact that, as the two of us had traveled, broken bread, and conversed and exchanged observations, feelings, and memories so extensively with our hosts, we had experienced such sincere kindnesses from them and had seen the love and compassion in their eyes as we all discussed brotherhood and the worth of souls. This surely was one of the great and special events in both our lives.

It was made very clear to us on that visit that, indeed, we are all God's children, all of us precious and divine in his sight, and we should desire and make every effort to build and strengthen one another.

Who are our enemies? Are they not children of God? Are they not our spiritual brothers and sisters? Are they not loved and cared for by the same benevolent being who watches over us all?

Who are we to hate our enemies when God our Father loves them? Who can suffer more at the hands of an enemy than did the Savior, who bore the sins of those who had mocked and scourged and finally crucified him? Whether they are enemies in the flesh or in the spirit, whether they seek to slay our bodies or our works, we can only follow the enticings of Jesus Christ if we want peace. We must be filled with his love if we hope to remove bitterness and fear from our lives.

A friend of mine passed through the fire of love and hate in his own way. He has given me permission to share the experience with you:

My father's cousin and my father lived in the same community and were competing in the construction business. There grew up over the years a very keen and bitter rivalry between them. This was triggered in the beginning in the bidding of construction contracts, and later in our city's political affairs where they opposed each other in very spirited elections.

Our immediate families inherited this situation upon the death of my father, for we boys [my father's sons] seemed to take over where Dad left off. It was quite a strain on the members of our families even to be civil to each other, even in our Church callings where my father's cousin eventually served as bishop of one ward and I in another, and later in the high council where we were both members. When we came together it seemed that Satan took over, and I am sure he did, for haven't we been told that where contention is, the Spirit of the Lord is not?

This situation continued to fester. Suddenly I found myself with a call to put aside all worldly things and go to preside over a mission. This was a thrilling experience to contemplate, and yet I subconsciously had a most uneasy feeling about it. I kept asking myself: "Are you really worthy to accept such an important call?" I was living the Word of Wisdom; I was a full tithe payer; I was faithful in all my Church activities; I was morally clean, and yet this uneasy feeling persisted.

I set about immediately to get my business and personal affairs in a condition where others could handle them while we were gone. While returning home from my office one afternoon, it really happened. I didn't hear a voice, but just as clearly as if a voice spoke to me something said: "You must go to your father's cousin and get things straightened out. You cannot go on this mission and teach the gospel of love when this terrible feeling exists between you."

I drove to his home, and with great fear and trepidation went up and rang the doorbell. There was no answer. After waiting a few minutes I went back to my car and said silently, "Lord, I made the attempt. I am sure this will be acceptable." But it wasn't. This uneasy feeling persisted. I prayed earnestly about it.

The next day as I sat in a funeral service, my cousin came in and sat across the aisle from me. The Spirit moved me to ask him if I could see him at his home after the service. He agreed. This time I went with calmness and tranquillity in my soul because I had asked the Lord to prepare the way for me. When I rang the doorbell he invited me into the living room and congratulated me on my mission call. We talked a few minutes about things in general, and then it happened. I looked at him with a feeling of love, which replaced all the old bitterness, and said: "I have come to ask forgiveness for anything I have ever said or done that has tended to divide us and our families."

At this point tears came into our eyes, and for a few minutes neither of us could say a word. This was one time when silence was more powerful than words. In a few minutes he said: "I wish I had come to you first."

I replied: "The important thing is that it is done, not who initiated it."

At this moment we had a rich spiritual experience, which caused us to purge our lives and our souls of those things which had separated us, which has resulted in our having proper family relationships.

Now I could go on my mission and teach the true meaning of love because for the first time in my life I had experienced its deepest dimension, and now I could honestly say that there wasn't a person in the world that I didn't love and appreciate. Since that day my life has never been the same, for it was then that I learned in a most positive way as I had never understood before the injunction of the Master to his disciples when he said: "A new commandment I give unto you, That ye love one another" (John 13:34).

Consider this little parable that teaches the power and at the same time the gentle persuasion of love:

"I'll master it," said the ax, and his blow fell heavily on the iron. But every blow made his edge more blunt and he finally ceased to strike.

"I'll show you the way," said the saw, "these teeth of mine will cut through anything." But the saw soon left the job defeated and broken.

"I'll show you the way," said the hammer. But after the first mighty blow, the iron remained unscarred.

"Shall I try?" said the soft, small flame. The ax, the saw, and the hammer all despised the flame, but the flame curled gently around the iron and embraced it until it melted under its influence.

There are hearts in men and women hard enough to resist the malice of wrath, the force of percussion, the fury of pride. But there is a power stronger than any of these, and hard indeed is the heart that can resist love.

—Author Unknown

Some of the most difficult battles we will ever fight will be on our knees. The battles of the soul, of the heart, determine who we are and what we will do in our lives, yet they are often fought silently, unnoticed by the world. To forgive others can be difficult, but to love all people whether they ask our forgiveness or not, whether they love us or not, can be among the greatest struggles we will ever face.

Love much. Earth has enough of bitter in it.
Cast sweets into its cup when e're you can.
No heart so hard that love, at last, may win it.

> Yes, love on, through doubt and darkness, and
> believe
> There is no thing which love may not achieve.
> —Author Unknown

Such Christlike love comes only through humility and through faith and hope, for it is a gift from the Master himself. If we have this love, this charity in Christ, we will love our spouses and children more unconditionally, our friends more completely, and our enemies absolutely. We may hate the evil of the world, but once we have conquered the battles in the heart, we will never hate another soul again.

Then, as we are filled with this love, we are prepared for the great and last promise the Lord makes to his Saints. As the hymn fervently entreats:

> Then when we have proven worthy
> Of thy sacrifice divine,
> Lord, let us regain thy presence;
> Let thy glory round us shine.

To Regain His Presence

And this is life eternal, that they might know thee the only true God, and Jesus Christ, whom thou hast sent.

—John 17:3

Part One

The knowledge of God is sacred. It is free to all, but it is also a gift from the divine. To say, "I know of God," is a good thing; it is the evidence of faith and the source of hope in Christ. But to say, "I *know* God," is the evidence of sacred revelation; it is the fruit of faith and the beginning of a perfect knowledge (see Alma 32:34).

In chapter one of this book, we suggested that one of the first attributes we need to develop in our efforts to find, stay close to, and return worthily to our Heavenly Father and his Son is that of a child-like faith. The statement was made in that first chapter that because children don't think they know everything, they are teachable. Throughout these pages we have tried to continue that thought, and we

87

especially emphasize it here, that coming to *know* God and his Son Jesus Christ necessitates a spirit of seeking and remaining teachable, humble, and full of faith. Children carry that spirit—they have an unwavering faith that accepts the reality of God and the mission of Christ, and they do so without doubting.

It's like the little four-year-old boy who, in company with his father, was taking his first ride on an express elevator in a high-rise building. As it zoomed upward, the boy, holding fast to his father's hand, looked up and said: "Daddy, does Heavenly Father know we're coming?"

Or the experience one family had while visiting in San Francisco. They attended a service in a large cathedral with its beautiful architecture and high ceilings. The small daughter of the family noticed a ladder inside that reached from the floor to the highest arch. Carefully studying the ladder for a few moments, she finally tugged at her father's sleeve and asked, "Daddy, is that the way you get to heaven and to Heavenly Father?"

Most members of the Church know of God. We have been taught of his attributes and physical reality. The scriptures and prophets testify of him. Most of our parents and leaders see to it that we are familiar with God's dealings with man in the Bible and Book of Mormon. We know that he appeared to Joseph Smith and restored the church of Christ on earth. But do we *know* him?

I had been raised in the Church and thought I knew him, but now I wonder if I really had. As a youth I wanted to play ball and date girls and have a good time. I prayed occasionally and learned the basics of the gospel, but I didn't spend too much time thinking about it. Then during a battle in World War II, hunkered down behind a low mound, I looked up to heaven. I was as scared as a man could be. "Are you there?" I pleaded. "I need help!"

Now, I don't know why, perhaps it was because this was the first time I had really prayed out loud sincerely, but the Spirit came upon me. I didn't see the Lord, but I knew, absolutely *knew*, that he was there. I heard no voice and saw no vision, but I had an assurance of his love and protection, of his absolute reality. I knew that he would preserve me and that if I did my part from then on, he would fulfill his promises as outlined in my patriarchal blessing. I knew in that moment that if I had had to, I could have stood up and walked through that blizzard of lead around me and not been hurt. Of course I didn't do that; I didn't need to prove the Lord. At that moment my knowledge of him was sure. My fear left me and never returned. Although I was concerned and anxious a few times, I never really feared death again.

In retrospect, I can see that that was the moment I began to *know* God. I had received a taste of what the prophets call "his matchless power." I had felt a portion of his love and knew that it was unshakable and also that it was more penetrating and more uplifting than any power I had known before. But this was just the beginning of knowledge for me. In a sense, it whetted my appetite. It made me want to discover more of this being who had truly been with me on that terrifying beach.

Elder David B. Haight, a member of the Council of the Twelve, shared the following:

> In the hearts of all mankind, of whatever race or station in life, there are inexpressible longings for something they do not now possess. This longing is implanted in man by a loving Creator. It is God's design that this longing of the human heart should lead to the one who alone is able to satisfy it. That fulness is found only in Jesus the Christ, the Son of our Eternal Father in Heaven. (*Ensign*, May 1982, p. 73)

We each have an inner "longing" to know our Savior again. It is part of our soul's basic makeup. But few of us, it seems, are able to satisfy this keen desire. Wherever we turn we see frustration and disappointment in the world. We see people hurting each other, striving for pleasure, wasting their lives and energy on things that do not bring peace. Could they be doing these things, perhaps in part, because they are frustrated in obtaining the one thing their souls truly long for? The love of Christ heals all things. A fullness of Christ will give the soul inexpressible joy—something, I believe, each of our spirits instinctively knows.

Many of these people in the world who are lashing out in frustration are actually good, wonderful souls. They're searching for answers. Some of them are asking, "Is he real? Can I trust in him?"

"The truth shall make you free," said the Savior (John 8:32), but you have to *know* the truth before that freedom can come.

A testimony is a spiritual verification that God lives, that Jesus is the Christ. It is also an affirmation that gospel principles are true and efficacious in our lives. This witness comes through the Holy Ghost. The principle of faith is based on this witness. Our testimonies of gospel truths can have great power, leading us to live by faith and to accomplish great things in the service of the Lord.

I never cease to marvel at the hundreds of profound thoughts given on all principles of truth and man's experience by great, humble, observant, and experienced men and women. It proves to me, and comfortingly so, that all through the ages of time mankind relives the same problems and continues to find that truth is the path toward the recognition and the solving of those problems.

When called to lead, the greatest blessing and privilege we have is to assist, motivate, and encourage our members not only to find and continually strengthen their testimonies, but to exert great energy in the wonderful and mighty work of coming to know the Savior. President Kimball so appropriately said of this most significant and valuable of life's goals: "Christ is our pattern, our guide, our prototype, and our friend. We seek to be like him so that we can always be with him" (*Ensign*, May 1979, p. 47).

When we know our Savior and seek to become like him, nothing can take the place of feeling his acceptance, his approval, his commendation of us and our efforts to obey his teachings and follow his counsel. We want to stay with him, serve him, and always be found worthy of his love. We try to do this, not because we feel it a duty, not because we fear him, but because we have learned from experience that to avoid wrongdoing and to embrace "principle" oriented living is to realize the natural peace, joy, and deep satisfaction that we all crave as human beings and which come from being in harmony with true principles.

Some on earth have been blessed with tremendous closeness to the Savior. What I share here, I do in deep reverence, in an awareness of the sacred nature of the experience. This account has been given before, but I relate it here to once again give a clear picture of the power of Jesus Christ and the hope we should have in living the principles he has taught us. This experience was given to Elder Melvin J. Ballard, an apostle of the Lord:

> I found myself one evening in the dreams of the night, in that sacred building, the Temple. After a season of prayer and rejoicing, I was informed that I should have the privilege of entering into one of those rooms, to meet a glorious Personage, and as I entered the door, I saw, seated on a raised platform the most glorious Being my eyes ever have beheld, or that I ever conceived existed in all the eternal worlds. As I approached to be introduced, he arose and stepped towards me with extended arms, and he smiled as he softly spoke my name. If I shall live to be a million years old, I shall never forget that smile. He took me into his arms and kissed me, pressed me to His bosom, and blessed me, until the marrow of my bones seemed to melt! When He had finished, I fell at His feet, and as I bathed them with my tears and kisses, I saw the prints of the nails in the feet of the Redeemer of the World. The feeling that I had in the presence of Him who hath all things in His hands, to have His love, His affection, and His blessings was such that if I ever can receive that of which I had but a foretaste, I would give all that I am, all that I ever hope to be, to feel what I then felt! (*The Faith of Our Pioneer Forefathers*, Bryant S. Hinckley, Salt Lake City: Deseret Book Co., 1956, pp. 226–27)

How powerful and sure Elder Ballard's knowledge of our Savior had become! No doubt his soul had hungered for this reunion, and he was filled, even if only with a "foretaste." Elder Haight has taught us that our spirits seek after this assurance of the Lord and that nothing but pure knowledge can satisfy this yearning in our souls.

Each of us, in time or in eternity, will meet with our Savior again. The final verse of the Book of Mormon leaves us with this promise:

> And now I bid unto all, farewell. I soon go to rest in the paradise of God, until my spirit and body shall again reunite, and I am brought forth triumphant through the air, to meet you before the pleasing bar of the great Jehovah, the Eternal Judge of both quick and dead. Amen. (Moro. 10:34)

When the time comes for us to be with the Savior again and to be judged according to our deeds in mortality, it could be a glorious occasion or one that could cause serious reflection. He should be our soul's desire. He is the embodiment of all that is good. He is life itself. President Gordon B. Hinckley bore this witness:

> None so great has ever walked the earth. None other has made a comparable sacrifice or granted a comparable blessing. He is the Savior and the

Redeemer of the world. I believe in Him. I declare His divinity without equivocation or compromise. I love Him. I speak His name in reverence and wonder. I worship Him as I worship His Father, in spirit and in truth. I thank Him and kneel before His wounded feet and hands and side, amazed at the love He offers me. (*Ensign*, Nov. 1986, pp. 50–51)

Can there be any doubt of President Hinckley's love for and knowledge of the Savior? What an example he has set for us in seeking and worshipping the Lord.

President Brigham Young taught: "The greatest and most important of all requirements of our Father in Heaven . . . is to believe in Jesus Christ, confess him, seek him, cling to him, make friends with him" (*Journal of Discourses*, 8:339).

Throughout this chapter we have discussed the tremendous importance of *knowing* the Father and the Son; of realizing the precious blessings and eternal effects that this knowledge can have in our lives; of recognizing the complete dependence we have on this truth for any lasting peace, joy, or success we will ever attain on this earth.

To the powerful and yet deeply humble testimonies of these truths borne by prophets and other leaders and recorded on these pages, we add the words of the Lord Jesus Christ himself, as he testified to the truthfulness of his Father's existence, glory, and Godhood and of his own. Knowing that he had finished his earthly mission, he prayed to the Father in behalf of his disciples and the Saints who would go on without his constant presence. "These words spake Jesus, and lifted up his eyes to heaven, and said, Father, the hour is come; glorify thy Son, that thy Son also may glorify thee: . . . And this is life eternal, that they might know thee the only true God, and Jesus Christ, whom thou hast sent" (John 17:1, 3).

How humbling it is to consider and to act upon the challenge given us through the example and words of great men and, above all, the very words of the Savior.

The life and experiences of the Prophet Joseph Smith, who was challenged himself, lend confidence and guidance as we strive to follow the counsel of our leaders.

Reflect a moment on the innocence and purity of a fourteen-year-old boy who was inspired and prompted to seek these same truths through the words of James, the very brother of Jesus, and who then sought God's will in a grove of trees. Joseph Smith and others in the Church were blessed with a great knowledge of the glory of God. They lived pure, humble lives and sought him earnestly. They lived for him. They were willing to die for him. Joseph left this answer for us before he laid down his life for the Lord:

How do men obtain a knowledge of the glory of God, his perfections and attributes? By devoting themselves to his service, through prayer and supplication incessantly strengthening their faith in him, until, like Enoch, the brother of Jared, and Moses, they obtain a manifestation of God to themselves. (*Lectures on Faith*, 2:55)

This manifestation may not come in the way that it came to Joseph or the brother of Jared. It may not come to the natural eyes or in the flesh. It may come more quietly, but just as certainly and powerfully. God knows each of his children, and he will speak to them according to their needs and faith.

And again, verily I say unto you that it is your privilege, and a promise I give unto you that have been ordained unto this ministry, that inasmuch as you strip yourselves from jealousies and fears, and humble yourselves before me, for ye are not sufficiently humble, the veil shall be rent and you shall see me and know that I am—not with the carnal neither natural mind, but with the spiritual. (D&C 67:10)

The Lord will speak to us in his own way, in his own time, according to his own will.

Part Two

Now, a word of caution. As you have contemplated the thoughts on these pages, if you, as we sincerely hope, feel the desire to follow the suggestions and counsel of great prophets, men of wisdom and humility who, themselves, have sought and have come to *know* God and his Son, and, indeed, the counsel and truths given by these same divine beings, you may have found a need for some personal life changes. Of course, the counsel, the testimonies, and personal experiences of great men are important as motivational tools, but they alone seldom give sufficient push to bring about difficult moral growth and development. It has been my own personal experience and that gleaned from years of counseling others that anytime life changes are needed, there are two powerful and fundamental principles included in the plan of salvation that must be understood. The two directly affect our thinking and our resulting behaviors, and confusion about their roles in our lives causes some to put off necessary and desired self-improvements. The first principle is that of opposition.

We are placed on this earth for a testing and probation of our souls, to see if we will keep our second estate. Trials will come to us that will tax us to the greatest degree possible. Although the Lord will not allow us to be tempted beyond that which we can bear, he will allow us to be stretched from time to time beyond that which we *thought* we could bear.

I remember so well the many times President Kimball talked and taught about the tragedies that occur in our lives. Quite often questions arose about untimely deaths of parents who left children behind or about missionaries who had died in the field. Some wondered why the Lord had not prevented the unfortunate occurrences. President Kimball had some profound insights into the subject of adversity. At one time he stated:

> Could the Lord have prevented these tragedies? The answer is yes. The Lord is omnipotent, with all power to control our lives, save us pain, prevent accidents, ... feed us, protect us, save us from labor, effort, sickness, even from death. But is that what you want? Would you completely shield your children from effort, from disappointments, temptations, sorrows, suffering? (*The Teachings of Spencer W. Kimball*, Bookcraft, 1982, p. 38.)

He went on to say that "the basic law is free agency. To force us to be careful or righteous would be to nullify that fundamental law, and growth would be impossible."

While speaking of our trials and adversities and the fact that we are on earth to be tested, it is good to realize that adversity is actually a form of opposition, or, better still, another definition of the word.

Opposition is a basic eternal law or principle which is a vital part of the plan of salvation.

The function of opposition as stated in the dictionary is "that which is or furnishes an obstacle to some result" or things "having contrasting tendencies." Any of our many and varied hardships and misfortunes, all the way from petty inconveniences to tragedies, are surely obstacles to our everyday peace and contentment and any progress we might be attempting to make. As such, opposition always causes us to have to *do* something—to move, to struggle, to think, to choose, to handle difficult situations—the list goes on. And that was probably the Lord's purpose for including the principle in his plan.

For a brief moment, let's go back to children again. Children have a positive and real feeling about heaven and the reality of a Heavenly Father when it comes to opposition—to struggling. A friend shared the following with me. His little daughter was trying again and again to keep her balance as she was learning to ride her new bike. When her dad gave her a big push, he overheard her saying, "Keep pushing, Jesus, and I'll do the pedaling." Stated again, opposition causes us to *do* something, and in the above case, the little daughter instinctively took the positive outlook, *doing* all she could by herself and asking the Lord to do the rest.

As most of us have discovered, if our lives were a constant flow of peaceful days, beauty, satisfaction, and good times, in other words "no strain, no pain," we could then quip, "no pain, no gain." And that's exactly what our lives would be—we would not progress, we would not grow, learn, change, nor, as a result, would we be as likely to find the Lord. There are some who don't turn to him at all, or they wait to do so until they are past desperation, until he is their last resort. Thus they miss some of the most comforting, helpful, and soul-satisfying experiences they could ever dream of having.

A short poem illustrates this thought.

> If your days were untroubled and your heart
>   always light, would you seek that fair land
>   where there is no night?
> If you never grew weary with the weight of your
>   load, would you search for God's peace at
>   the end of the road?
> If you never knew sickness and never felt pain,
>   would you reach for a hand to help and
>   sustain?
> If all you desired was yours day by day, would you
>   kneel before God and earnestly pray?
>   —Author Unknown

This realistic and thought-provoking portrayal of the role of opposition in our lives reminds me of the humorous account of a young Primary student who was counseled by his teacher to remember each night to kneel beside his bed in prayer. The boy's answer was, "If I chose to do that, there would have to be a real miracle. I sleep on the top bunk."

Returning back to the verse quoted above, we know, then, from our own personal experience, that adversity—opposition—if handled with the proper attitude, can provide a path to moral growth and strength that nothing else can. And, though it may be difficult to live with, opposition is a necessary component of earth life.

Brigham Young said, "The Prophet Joseph Smith was more perfect in thirty-eight years with the severe tribulation through which he passed, than he would have been in one thousand years without it."

Considering opposition, which always causes some kind of action on our part, we are led to the second fundamental principle that I feel is so important to understand as part of the plan of salvation, that of free agency. This most basic and vital principle, one of the first and key factors that governs man's existence on earth, is directly and indispensibly related to the adversities and trials that we must endure throughout our lives. We must appreciate this fact as we view earth life and the life to come.

The forces of opposition allow us the opportunity, indeed, the obligation, to use this God-given gift of agency to choose between good and evil, right and wrong. But it is important to understand that the nature of free agency dictates that our choices will inevitably bring about consequences, good or bad, depending upon the many decisions we make. Now, right here, ponder this question. Would not an all-knowing, all-wise Eternal Father, himself bound by absolute respect for and adherence to all eternal law, want his children to learn from their own mistakes, mistakes they make through ignorance, even innocence, or especially through willful, deliberate wrongdoing? Perhaps learning "the hard way" is the best teacher of all! This lesson was learned by an important businessman in a certain community.

> "What is the secret of your success?" a reporter asked a bank president.
> "Two words."
> "And what would they be, sir?"
> "Right decisions."
> "And how do you make right decisions?"
> "Experience."
> "And how do you get experience?"
> "Two words."
> "What are they?"
> "Wrong decisions."

In light of our agency, it seems, then, that the Lord doesn't have to cause or send us problems. He

may simply allow them to occur. All he really needs
to do is honor the regrettable choices we ourselves
make and those made by our fellow human beings,
decisions which often effect us negatively, and the
tribulations and adversities will soon follow as natural consequences of our acts—and in as many different forms, probably, as there are individuals.
There is also another source of challenge and
adversity that has nothing to do with choices, that
being the forces of nature over which no man has
complete control. Finally, it is wise to recall that
the types of tribulations we have are immaterial.
What matters is how we deal with each one.

The Lord's purpose for man is that he become
like his Father, and to do this he must develop the
virtue of personal responsibility for his decisions,
his thoughts, his actions, and whatever consequences result. It follows, then, that if he has the
freedom to choose, he can in fairness be held
accountable for those choices.

Keep in mind as well, that despite our mistakes,
the Lord will be merciful. If we are constantly striving to please him, even if we seem to fall short, he
will attend us with his love and divine grace. It is
not required that we become perfect in every way in
this life. If it were, only one perfect Being would
have been saved. I recall my father often saying to
me, "Paul, remember that there is no all at once;
perfection is an ongoing process." I'm sure the man

who asked the Lord for his help with the following would be relieved. He prayed: "Dear God, please help me be the person my dog thinks I am."

Several meaningful statements made by the prophets and others who have learned through personal experiences reveal how we should appreciate the great blessing of free agency and its use as a testing medium for mankind.

• "Therefore, cheer up your hearts, and remember that ye are free to act for yourselves—to choose the way of everlasting death or the way of eternal life" (2 Ne. 10:23).

• "And now remember, remember, my brethren, that whosoever perisheth, perisheth unto himself; and whosoever doeth iniquity, doeth it unto himself; for behold, ye are free; ye are permitted to act for yourselves; for behold, God hath given unto you a knowledge and he hath made you free" (Hel. 14:30).

• President David O. McKay continually reminded us that "a fundamental principle of the gospel is free agency, and references in the scriptures show that this principle is (1) essential to man's salvation; and (2) it may become a measuring rod by which the actions of men, of organizations, of nations may be judged."

• He also said, "Without this divine power to choose, humanity cannot progress" (Conference Report, October 1965, pp. 7–8).

• Free agency, combined with respect for eternal law, gives us the privilege of designing for ourselves almost any kind of life situation, mind set, and attitude that we desire. It is an imperative key to repentance and to our ultimate destiny in the post-mortal world. But this means that we must choose to meet the conditions necessary for eternal life.

• The greatest suffering of the world might be traced to the unholy, destructive doctrine that man need not conform to law, whether of man, nature, or God.

• Keep in mind that the only true freedom is that of living within the law.

• If something is done, a definite result follows. If something is desired, certain definite things must be done.

How grateful we all can be for the atoning sacrifice of our Lord and for his willingness to seek after us constantly. It is because of his sacrifice that we can use our agency to choose eternal life, the kind and quality of life that God the Father and his Son experience. While we are weak, they are strong. The Savior is the rock upon which we build our foundation. Helaman, speaking to his sons, taught this basic truth:

> And now, my sons, remember, remember, that it is upon the rock of our Redeemer, who is Christ, the Son of God, that ye must build your foundation; that when the devil shall send forth his mighty winds, yea, his shafts in the whirlwind, yea, when all his hail and his mighty storm shall beat upon you, it shall have no power over you to drag you down to the gulf of misery and endless woe, because of the rock upon which ye are built, which is a sure foundation, a foundation whereon if men build they cannot fall. (Hel. 5:12)

To have the Savior as our foundation equips us with strength and power to overcome adversity and to accept his atoning sacrifice, which is God's greatest gift to us. While we will never comprehend the Atonement fully on this earth, it promises resurrection to all and, in addition, exaltation to those who live God's commandments, participate in the principle of repentance, and become worthy to live in his presence. The Savior freely accomplished the hardest part. In so doing he introduced the principle of mercy, which means doing for us that which we could not do for ourselves.

In the New Testament, Christ gives us, through the book of Revelation, a promise and a challenge:

> Behold, I stand at the door, and knock: if any man hear my voice, and open the door, I will come in to him, and will sup with him, and he with me.
>
> To him that overcometh will I grant to sit with me in my throne, even as I also overcame, and am set down with my Father in his throne. (3:20–21)

With gratitude and deep humility, I testify that I *know* the Savior. I have undeniably felt his love for me, and I rejoice that he is my friend. My spiritual experiences with him are precious and sacred to me, and I will be forever grateful for each one. My knowledge and conviction of his reality and his Sonship do not waver, and his tender love has attended and comforted me throughout my life.

I realize and accept the fact that I will not be perfect in this life, but I appreciate each new day as an opportunity to build inner strength and strive towards a more complete understanding of Christ's atoning sacrifice on the way to living with him once more. I love the Savior. He is my friend, and I look forward to the day when we shall all be readmitted into his presence. May this be the hope and realization of all of us.

Conclusion—
Let Thy Glory Round Us Shine

*For the Lord shall be in their midst, and his glory shall be
upon them, and he will be their king and their lawgiver.*

—D&C 45:59

As I noted in the introduction, each of us comes to
this life on earth after having experienced a premortal conflict. Indeed, it might be said that, from
the very outset, we are soldiers in a royal army—
with no way to avoid all the slings and arrows of the
adversary, the "bullets and shrapnel" of the world.
And this "battle of mortality," which begins at the
time of our birth, is at the same time an unequaled
blessing, one for which we shouted with joy.

Thus, regardless of the type of encounter, we
fight for our lives, our beliefs, our hopes, and our
dreams. Exaltation is the goal. Inevitably, along the
way we will win some battles and lose others, but
hopefully we will be victorious in winning those
that lead to our goal. Failure lies not in losing the
daily battles, but in giving up the long fight.

The secret to this success, I believe, is that certain something within us that does not allow us to despair. In my own life that something is my faith in God, which has compelled me to press forward. It has allowed me to feel comfort in bitter times and to try to comfort others in their distress. In the midst of tribulation, such confidence and security have come from the knowledge that I am nothing without my friend and Savior, but that with him I am capable of enduring and winning all the battles in this life.

As mentioned earlier, my tools and tactics have changed over the years. Trying to follow my father's counsel to fight the battles of mortality on the Lord's ground and not the world's, I fight today by working, praying, repenting, listening, and trying to be of service to others. The rewards of winning our battles in the Lord's way are sure: "even peace in this world and eternal life in the world to come" (D&C 59:23). The greatest victory is conquering self rather than others.

It is not required that we become perfect all at once. In fact, in this life, it will not happen. But in humility, with our Savior, all things are possible.

Index

plan of salvation, x
positive outlook, 68–70,
  74–75
praise, 69, 76
prayer, 19–20, 89
pre-earth life, ix, x
prejudice, 55–58
pride, 40, 65
progression, 101
prophets, humility of, 3–5,
  9–18; love of, 67–68

R

Rabbi Ben, story, 53–58
relationships, 65, 84
repentance, 46, 98
revelation, receiving, 20

S

Samuel, 51–52
Satan, ix–x
Smith, Hyrum, 38–39
Smith, Joseph, x, 17, 37,
  38–39, 70, 96, 97, 102
Solomon, 53
Spirit, learning language of,
  34

T

Taylor, John, 19
teachable, 1, 88
temple marriage, 28, 30–34
temptation, x, 98–99
testimony, 89, 91
tolerance, 47–66
trials, x, xi, 17, 98–100, 102

U

understanding, 53, 61

W

war in heaven, ix–x
weakness, 3, 34, 46
woman taken in adultery,
  58–59
worthiness, 28, 30–34

Y

Young, Brigham, 37–38, 95

Z

Zacchaeus, 49–50